IN WOMEN WE TRUST

A cultural shift to the softer side of business

Mary Clare Hunt

WME BOOKS
a division of
Windsor Media Enterprises, LLC
Rochester, New York
USA

IN WOMEN WE TRUST
A cultural shift to the softer side of business

Copyright © 2006 by Mary Clare Hunt
All rights reserved. Printed in USA.

ISBN 0-9777297-2-9

Cover Design: Maria G. Farrell
Page Layout/Design: Tom Collins

Published by:
    WME Books
    Windsor Media Enterprises, LLC
    Rochester, New York
    USA

Available online at: **www.WMEBooks.com**
as well as other booksellers and distributors worldwide

Special Sales:
This and other WME Books titles are available at special discounts for bulk purchases, for use in sales promotions, or as premiums. Special editions, including personalized covers, excerpts of existing books, and corporate imprints, can be created in large quantities for special needs or projects.

For more information, please contact:
Special Book Orders
Windsor Media Enterprises, LLC
282 Ballad Avenue
Rochester, NY 14626

1-877-947-BOOK (2665)

info@wmebooks.com

Dedication

To my husband Mike,
whose intellect
and love
inspire me daily.

Acknowledgements

I consider this book a continuation of "the discussion" started by a number of women offering some unique takes on the subject of women and marketing. Michelle Miller helped get our brains around the gender issue with her book, *The Natural Advantages of Women*. Martha Barletta provided a compass to keep marketing departments heading in the right direction in her book, *Marketing to Women*. Lisa Johnson and Andrea Learned taught us to think in transparent terms in *Don't Think Pink*. Yvonne DiVita took the discussion online in *Dickless Marketing*. And Judy Rosener pointed to the fastest solution back in 1995 with *America's Competitive Secret: Women Managers*. Their contributions form a knowledge baseline for business.

Since no buyer/seller conversation is one sided, I would also like to thank the many voices who contributed to the consumer side of this book. Their candid viewpoints bring the message alive for those working outside of the marketing departments. Vicky, Kate, Martha, Judy, Dee, Charlene, Patty, Rebecca, Andrea, Maria, Sue, Celeste, Jana, Jill and the many friends they brought to the conversation as well as the members of WomanSage and Awesome-Women, my gratitude to you all. Although I scrambled your personas to protect your privacy you'll recognize yourselves throughout the chapters.

A special thank you goes to those who added balance to the book. To Rick, Mark and Mike whose comments kept me in check, and especially to my business partner Terri Whitesel for her ongoing insights and life experiences.

Lastly, my sincere appreciation to Yvonne and Tom for their publishing patience and Maria for wrapping it all in a classic cover design. This wouldn't have happened without your encouragement and support.

Table of Contents

Introduction	1
1 - The Women's Consumer Culture Is Shifting	5
2 - Money – and Motive – Talks	17
3 - Women: the Mega Market with the Megaphone	23
4 - In Women We Trust, to Show Us *Their* Way	31
5 - The Community Spirit of Like-Minded Friends	41
6 - Respectful of Her Background and Ideas	53
7 - Considerate of Her Needs	69
8 - Fun and Inspiring to be Around	81
9 - Safe to be "Me" with You	91
10 - Honest with Her from the Beginning	105
11 - Reliable Beyond Question	119
12 - Thoughtful of Others in Her Global Community	133
13 - Loyalty, the Sum Total of the Trust Points	149
In Women We Trust. In Business We Hope.	161
Appendices	
Index	

Introduction

"Who's your audience?"

That's what everyone asked when I first started writing this book. "Are you trying to create awareness for business or for female consumers?"

"Both," was my reply. You can't have a strong offering without a strong support base and you can't have a strong support base if women don't trust you enough to even sample the offering.

Women may fall in and out of love, but they don't fall in and out of trust.

Business has been slicing and dicing their customers by their demographics and then mass marketing to them for years. Today consumers are slicing and dicing them back making decisions based on who they can trust long before they see an offering. Both are playing new roles in the interlinked marketplace where the consumer is queen. Thereby each side needs awareness of how the other one thinks.

Smart marketers already know that women are in the decision seat when it comes to purchasing 80% of consumer products and services. What they may not know is that these same women are taking a lot more into account than just the offering, especially if there is face-to-face interaction as in professional services or sales.

Smart women already know that their power is rising in the marketplace: one look at the number of commercials showing everyday women's faces tells them that. What they may not know is how their voice, writings, and actions are rocking the consumer world.

What could surprise both is an early indicator that women are choosing woman-based services because they trust the culture (in general) that women provide. This is especially prevalent in midlife women who have had a lifetime of working with both genders and are now putting their money with their friends or where their friends tell them to put it. Coming along with them are their daughters who are seeking advice from "mom" or each other online.

So what exactly do women offer other women? Why does the trust factor lead to an assumed trust level between them? How can business apply the same values and keep both genders as customers?

We'll attempt to answer those questions and also leave you with more of your own to ask the women in your business life.

 *Introduction*

This book is for marketers who aren't yet aware of the culture shift, for employees who can influence customers more than advertising and to the female consumers who take their purchasing power seriously, using it to help companies find their footing.

In women we trust, to show business their way.

1 The Women's Consumer Culture Is Shifting ...

It's a slow, silent shift – like the melting of the ice caps – but one that in its own way could melt down centuries of social systems. Women are opting to work with their own "culture" first – in a quiet, under-the-radar defection to the softer side of business.

Why are they doing it?

The answer is because they can (if they want to), and the reality is – they want to. Fear not, they aren't leaving men behind, just the traditional corporate mindset, in pursuit of one that suits them better. Companies don't have to be all female to re-capture this group; they need only to supply goods and services in a way that closely mimics the culture their female customers use outside of business, in their daily lives.

> *Women are opting to work with their own "culture" first.*

Ladies First

My curiosity about this whole "women's culture" thing was piqued after taking a survey of baby boomer women in Southern California – the ones who own their homes, have a full-time career or retirement savings, expendable incomes and who have lived through decades of social change.

I asked, **"If all things are equal and competency isn't a factor, do you prefer to use women or men for your professional services, for example: CPA, doctor, financial planner, lawyer, etc."** The majority of respondents said, "Women," but not because they wanted to support the sisterhood; they simply felt more comfortable with women for many of the reasons they give below. Even those women who stated that competency, not gender, was their first criteria, said that they went with the person whom they felt "cared about them" or was a part of their circle of friends.

> "I feel like the female doctors I've had, now and in the past, listen and actually care about what's happening to me."
>
> Realtor, age 54

> "Through the years the women I have worked with seem to be more responsive and also gave me more work for the dollar."
>
> Former software programmer, age 62

> "My preference would be female, only because I feel that they would watch out for me more than a man would."
>
> Franchise business owner, age 51

> "I prefer females as I have found they generally are more detail oriented, more patient, easier to communicate with and more honest. However, I still think sometimes it depends on the individual. Actually, two yours ago my 90 year old mother

> brought it to my attention first – she said that she trusted women professionals more and got better service."
>
> Accountant, age 55
>
> "I would say overall that as time goes on I am progressively using more and more women to provide care and services. I would not switch back to a male for my primary medical care and would take my HMO to task if they decided to assign me one. I do prefer to work with women which I did in the field that I chose. Occasionally, I did work with men who were vendors but preferred working with women whenever possible. They seem better organized and dependable and usually it is easier to communicate with a woman."
>
> Former hospital employee, age 66

Wow! That was an eye opener. Companies trying to tap the female market via new offerings and messages aren't seeing how women are quietly choosing their own culture before viewing even one brochure. For these women, it is no longer a choice between a professional man or a professional woman. For the majority of them, the choice is between professional women.

It's important to restate that none of the women surveyed said that men were incompetent; competency was a "given" in the equation. The "currency" was an ability to trust and get along with the person across the desk; the women needed more than a friendly face: it had to be someone who would care about them, take time to listen, and would work in their best interest.

Their years of experience working with both men and women told our midlife survey takers the same thing: that women had more of the qualities they wanted, and therefore the female culture was now getting the first nod. It's almost as if the female culture had become a "brand."

Gal Pals Unite:
New Organizations on the Grow

I then checked around to see if other defections were occurring; was it a fluke of the times, or a serious market trend?

In the *Directory of Orange County Networking Organizations*, which lists over 680 professional and social groups, the number of women's groups is so large it has its own tabbed section. It's human nature to prefer working with people you can relate to on an emotional level; in this case these women are getting to know a lot of other women first.

- One of biggest groups is the **The Red Hat Society**, headquartered in Fullerton, CA. Now in its seventh year, this group has 41,000 chapters and over one million members, across 29 countries. Red Hats are party people – grab your gal pals, purple dress/red hat and go have fun. You can't miss their flashy attire at any public event, and that's just the point, they don't care that they stand out. They wear their confidence proudly and they're getting to know many others just as wild as they are, over lunch.

- Another new social group is **WomanSage**, with a mission to "Enrich, Empower, and Educate" midlife women. They don't promote business-to-business networking, but it happens anyway. WomanSage started with 30 women talking about issues they all faced at midlife, and a year later they had 400 women in their Orange County group. They are now building nationwide chapters. Their popularity comes from tapping into a market segment that wasn't being served, women who were formally expected to go quietly into retirement.

- Other organizations are more business-driven, like **ewomanetwork.com** with 80 chapters and 800,000 members. They bill themselves as the "#1 resource for promoting women and their business." Ewomanetwork has physical meetings but its power comes from its virtual networking between women.

These three organizations alone are each less than seven years old and have close to two million active members. The critical factor is that they are meeting face-to-face as well as online. Members get to know and trust one another and friendships turn into business or are a conduit to helping others who might need their services.

Older Organizations Regroup

That speaks to the emerging interests, but what about older groups – the ones that were started decades ago when women weren't allowed into the "men only" associations? With today's more gender-neutral society you would think that these women's associations would fade and rejoin the mainline group, *but that isn't happening.*

For trend watchers, it's no longer important to know why they formed, only that these older groups are still here today and growing. The question is, "What are the women able to get from female-based groups that they can't get in the mixed gender group?" These aren't wimpy women getting together to rag about the inequality in the workplace, these are mainliners who have moved on to mainline issues.

- American Business Women's Association
- American Society of Women Accountants
- Association for Women in Technology
- Commercial Real Estate Women
- California Women's Leadership Association
- Executive Women International
- Financial Women International
- Forum for Women Entrepreneurs
- National Association of Professional Mortgage Women
- National Association of Women Business Owners
- National Association of Women in Construction
- Women Lawyers Association
- Society of Women Engineers
- Women in Cable & Telecommunications
- Women in International Trade
- Women in Management
- Women Manufacturers Network

and many more…

1 The Women's Consumer Culture is Shifting

Taking on (their own) Business

Thanks to higher education and other social advances, such as being able to secure better bank loans, women are buying and running their own companies at an enormous rate. At this writing, **women own 9.2 million or 46% of all companies in America and employ more people than the Fortune 500.** Many of these companies were formed when women gave up trying to be part of the "corporate culture." Rather than pound on the glass ceiling, they started their own companies creating their own "culture."

They're doing a great job, too. **Statistically more women-owned start-up companies are making it past the five year mark than male-owned start-ups.** That's important from both an investment and sales point of view as the businesses appear more stable at the beginning of a growth curve.

We also know that the majority of those woman-owned businesses are service based, either as a business offering or as a way of keeping customers. Nurturing and taking care of others is what women do best – operating a business that *serves customers well* is simply an extension of that. It's all a part of women's culture.

What's the bottom line? **Those 9.2 million companies represent a lot of computers, desks, raw materials, office supplies, and employee benefits.** Who will these women be turning to when they need to buy products and services? From the looks of the survey and the groups they hang out with, it'll be from the other women or *a business culture that resonates with them whether it's woman-owned or not.*

Taking Back Their Lives

If you look at three areas of "choice" so far, in each case women are opting for a path of least frustration:

- For their personal business needs, they are looking for someone they feel they can trust and talk to.
- In groups, they are turning to others for fun as well as a way to learn new things.
- By starting their own businesses, they are eliminating the frustration of not being promoted or of not being hired because they are too old or took time off to be a mom.

Add to that list: choosing a single lifestyle.

In today's world it doesn't shock anyone to hear that 50% of marriages fail. Forty years ago, it was more like 25%. Clearly something has changed; that change is that women now have the economic means and personal confidence that gives them a choice between staying put or moving on. What is more surprising is that it's happening even in very long term marriages. According to a study of divorced couples over 40 by the AARP, **66% of the divorces were initiated by the women.**

> "I prefer [to work with] women, they are more respectful of me."
> Newly divorced woman after 23 years of marriage, age 52

That's a sobering statement, but one that is critical to the psychological profile of today's female customer. It shows what women are willing to do to eliminate the frustration of failed relationships regardless of their "promise" or decades of commitment time.

1 The Women's Consumer Culture is Shifting

Divorce doesn't turn women off to men; the dating sites are full of both male and female divorcees looking for another chance at love. But it will factor into how women relate to others in the future. It also affects their gal pals, since those pals are the ones providing emotional support during and after the divorce. You can't have something as emotionally charged as divorce happening to half the population and not have some new, personal rules being written.

According to Barnes and Noble, 80% of customers who buy books on relationships are women. Some may say that proves that women need more help than men. Others would argue that the women are taking charge of their lives, to learn what's going right or going wrong, in an effort to avoid making the same mistakes again and again.

> *80% of customers who buy books on relationships are women.*

Regardless of whether you see it as a sign of weakness or strength, it shows how deeply and emotionally women are reacting to the building of a "relationship." They are the ones willing to research it, before, during and after. What they learn during that process gets fed into their personality mix and can't be ignored later on because "it's just business" – a common male assertion. What the women feel and learn goes with them.

Shift Happens ... Will This One Lock In?

I think so, even if this is at the beginning of the curve.

If women are choosing professional services offered by other women, having fun with their own kind, starting their own businesses and leaving long-term marriages, (or choosing to stay single), then companies who want a competitive edge will need to fit into "their culture" first, before promoting their business.

We, at Interpret-her, are already seeing this happening in niche places, such as the professional services areas, but those niches are showing such promise that smart companies will want to follow suit. Competition for a woman's mindshare will happen on a much deeper level and one that travels throughout the entire company. Just like you can't add "quality" at the end of a production line, you can't add "female-friendliness" at the end, either. A true female-friendly culture washes over the entire company to the point that it becomes transparent.

> *A true female-friendly culture washes over the entire company to the point that it becomes transparent.*

To go back to the original survey question, "Who would they choose, men or women?" the underlying deciding point was who would they trust with their most personal issues – those things that affected their very existence, such as, health, finance and legal matters?

1   The Women's Consumer Culture is Shifting

After finding that "women" are who they would trust, our next question becomes, "What exactly is it that they are trusting sight unseen?" And further, "What can we learn about the female experience that can be implemented in companies?" Women trust other women now, only because they don't see enough choices that can provide the same "trust values."

Will companies be able to match up to their value system?

Is a trip along another learning curve worth it?

In the next couple of chapters we'll give you a snapshot of the numbers and how the market is changing over to one that is based on word-of-mouth integrity, and we'll let you decide.

2 Money – and Motive – Talks

Thanks to linked databases and social networking, companies can now prove what most women have known for a long time: women make or will influence the decision on over 80% of all consumer purchases. Whether they are earning the money or not isn't the point. The key phrase is "make or influence" the decision.

Women are either buying products or services for themselves, purchasing them for their family members or influencing the decision from the home front. In the last case, you may not see the woman, but she has already had her say and that will affect what the family member in front of you is buying. To put it another way, she's the one who gave them the list.

> *You may not see the woman, but she has already had her say.*

So what happened? Why are big and small companies just starting to acknowledge a women's purchasing role in the market? The answer: Awareness followed by economics.

Seeing women as an active consumer isn't about being socially or politically correct the way it was in the 60s; it's about making a profitable business decision. Profitable business decisions are made by following the money.

Baby Boomers, Their Daughters and Their Friends

Here's a snapshot of this female market.

Women are the majority of consumers:
- The U.S. Census showed in 2000 that there were 267,636,000 people in the US; 50.5% of them are women.
- 47% of all adult women are single, divorced or widowed; of that group, 40% are over age 40.
- Women are guiding trillions in purchasing:
  - $3.7 trillion in consumer spending.
  - $1.5 trillion in business spending.

They make (or influence) decisions on everything:
- 83% of all consumer products and services.
- 91% of all new homes.
- 50-60% of all auto purchases.

- 89% of the bank accounts.
- 93% of the food.
- 88% of the kitchen appliances.
- 51% of consumer electronics. (Of the $96 billion spent on electronics in 2003, $55 billion was spent by women.)
- 80% of family health care spending.
- 60% of adult care giving.
- 81% of the riding lawn mowers.
- 21% of single women buy a home vs. 11% of single men.
- 51% of total travel market.

How did they get all that cash and clout? Since 1970, the female workforce has doubled to 67 million, with education playing a key role in the choice of good paying jobs.

Women hold:
- 56% of bachelor degrees.
- 57% of masters' degrees.
- 42% of doctorate degrees.
- 60% of accounting/auditing positions.
- 22% of industrial engineer's positions.

Women are earning degrees in traditionally male-dominated fields:
- 46% of all law school students.
- 43% of all veterinary students.
- 43% of all medical students.

They manage the money they have:
- 48% of stock market investors are women.
- 47% of all investors with assets over $100,000 are women.
- Women investors have outperformed male investors nine out of the last 12 years.
- 42% of households with assets greater than $600,000 are headed by women.
- The amount of money that will pass through women's hands between 2010 and 2015 is projected to be $12.5 trillion.
- In 34% of married households, the women who work outside of the home earn more than their husbands.
- Women earn $1 trillion dollars a year.

They run their own businesses:
- Women-owned businesses comprise 46% of ALL companies in this country, over 9.2 million total.
- They generate $1.2 trillion in sales.
- 1987 to 1999 the number of women-owned businesses grew 103%, or one and one-half times the national average.
- Their employment levels grew 320%.
- Their revenues grew 436%.
- They employ 18 million people.
- The fastest growing women owned businesses were the larger companies – those with over 100 employees.

- They buy $44.5 billion in office supplies.
- By end of 2005, made up 50% of the business travel market.
- Women-owned businesses are most successful in the same top 5 fields as male-owned businesses:
    1. Manufacturing
    2. Wholesale
    3. Services
    4. Retail
    5. Construction

Sources:
www.ewowfacts.com 2004
Men's Health http://www.menshealth.com
Consumer Electronics Association 2003
Bank Marketing International
Women's Financial Network
American Association of Retired Persons
"What Women Really Want," *Free Press*, October 2005

The Everyday Woman Made It Happen

The early 1960s movement, made up of thousands of women's voices and actions, coupled with the actions and voices of today's outspoken ladies, are what made those big numbers possible. Just a bunch of average students, wives, and mothers – carrying signs or writing editors, or calling radio shows.

For example: Until 1972, girls weren't allowed to participate equally in high school sponsored sports or educational programs. That changed when Title IX was first proposed and then approved, giving girls the same developmental opportunities as boys.

As those young women started breaking down the stereotypes of what could be done athletically and academically, their dedication and spirit inspired both peers and older women to do better. That spirit was carried with them into college, into their personal lives, and finally, into business.

That's an important element to consider; because now those same women are today's midlifers – a very large group of women who still aren't afraid to speak their minds. Their Gen X and Gen Y daughters – who grew up with Title IX – don't even question their space on the planet; they "own" it. While midlife women are torn between the old ways and the new ways, these new generations of women do it "their" way without hesitation. All age groups are just beginning to understand their power as active consumers and the effect their choices make. The more aware they become, the more business will need to align with them on a deeper level.

3 Women: The Mega Market with the Megaphone

Selling to one woman would be reason enough to learn how to work within their culture, but you're never selling to "one." Let's face it, women like to talk about their lives, things, places, careers. Some people call that "gossip."

In the past, "gossip" (spreading ideas from one person to another) was considered a worthless expenditure of time. Today, gossip has been relabeled as "word-of-mouth" marketing (WOM), and it is a coveted asset. When word-of-mouth is spreading the good word, it's free advertising. But, if your product and/or service is shoddy, word-of-mouth becomes something else entirely. While women may not tell you personally, they will warn others – that's when the free may turn costly in lost revenue and reputation.

> *Word-of-mouth may become something else entirely.*

WOM - The Women's Media

Admit it. When you saw the word "gossip," which culture came to mind first, male or female? Almost everyone would say female even though studies show that men gossip as much as women. There is a difference between male and female gossip, according to a report by Kate Fox titled, "Evolution, Alienation and Gossip," from the Social Issues Research Center at Oxford:

> The research indicates moms are among the most active people online, discussing every aspect of their lives, and reviewing and recommending hundreds of different products.
>
> Auto-brand conversation among moms ranks third; greater than for cereal brands but below that of baby food and retail shopping venues.
> Source: BuzzMetrics

- Men talk more about themselves.
- Men talk to men *and* women, while women prefer to talk primarily with women.

Those are important differences if you have a product or service you want chatted up in the marketplace. Who will talk it up more: those who are talking about themselves or those who are talking about the product?

Why Is It that Women Talk to Women More?

In that same report, gossip is described as social grooming, or a way women relate to one another and test our social boundaries. Talking with others releases endorphins and oxytocin relieving stress and boosting the immune system. It's essential to our social, psychological and physical well-being.

3 ✹ Women: The Mega Market with the Megaphone

For women, gossiping and/or talking is considered entertainment. Part of that is the response we get – usually in highly animated tones, with plenty of detail and enthusiasm, which women provide and men generally don't. It doesn't take long to understand why women turn to other women when they need some social grooming. They go to the people who reciprocate their enthusiasm: other women who give energy as good as they get energy.

You don't need a study from Oxford to tell you that women are better at word-of-mouth. Go to any small town and observe who is doing the talking *and connecting*. Small towns cut to the basics of human interaction. The town leaders may be giving directions, but the town women are setting up the church banquets, taking care of families during funerals, seeing to the sick and attending the school plays. The women are the glue that holds the small town neighborhood, or even the small town office, together. Because they talk and stay connected they are often the first to know when problems happen.

It's our culture to watch over one another and pitch in to help until the crisis or event is past. It's our culture to be "in the know," not so much to be nosey but because it makes us part of the group. Talking to one another builds relationships, bonds groups together, clarifies social positions, and reinforces shared values.

{ *Talking to one another builds relationships...* }

Staying connected

Talking increases when you add tools such as mail, phone, emails and social software like blogs.

Who in today's world has the bigger address books, holiday and birthday card lists? Men or Women?

Who is on the phone more? Men or Women?

Who gets the most personal e-mail? Men or Women?

Who has more friends "copied" on every emailed joke? Men or Women?

> What do women do online for entertainment? The highest scoring item was "e-mailing" at 82%.
> Source: E-Marketer, May 2005 "Women online in the US"

What about blogs, discussion boards, forums, instant messaging? Who will dominate that space? At the time of this printing, it's about 50/50 depending on what survey you read, but if what we know about the offline world holds true, then the online world will soon follow. Men may "discuss themselves and things," but if above is any indication, women are the biggest transferees of information.

The "Canaries" of Commerce

Authors Ed Keller and Jon Berry of *The Influencers*, focus on finding the "key" people in a market who can start a chain reaction from being aware of a product to endorsing it among consumers. These key people – like

3 ❀ Women: The Mega Market with the Megaphone

Oprah or Martha Stewart – are considered mega hubs, as they can influence millions of other women. Others argue that it's those in between the hubs who are the real word-spreaders.

In the best situations, it's both. But neither can happen unless A) someone talks; and B) someone shares the information.

The president of KN™ Pajamas, Karen Neuberger, says that being featured on "Oprah's Favorite Things" program is what kick-started her pajama line. But that selling spurt would have been short-lived if the sleepwear wasn't something that all women loved and raved about to others. Oprah may have started the idea, but everyday women carried it forward.

> "We've found that 80 percent of every WOM interaction takes place face-to-face."
>
> Dave Balter, BuzzAgent

Their Voice, Activated

The Internet gives women a 'voice' in the social process, a voice they never had before. No longer are they caught behind "permission-based road blocks," such as getting a degree and a job before writing for a magazine or newspaper. They no longer have to hope their letters to the editor get approved and printed, or that their complaint letter gets seen by the CEO. Today's women can search for an infinite number of blogs, discussion

> *No longer are they caught behind permission-based road blocks.*

boards, or feedback sites such as www.planetfeedback.com, www.epinions.com, www.ripoffreport.com, or Intuit's latest addition, www.zipingo.com, and in two seconds post their complaint or comment live, for the entire world to see. (See Appendix A.)

Just 10 years ago, such complaint letters may have seen a circular file, now they are a permanent part of the Internet memory – for everyone to read again and again.

WOM + Women, Try and Stop it

According to consulting giant McKinsey, "About two-thirds of all economic activity in the US is influenced by shared opinions about a product, brand or service …word-of-mouth as a marketing discipline is only just coming into its own, and the data indicate its best years are yet to come."

> Out of 12 kinds of advertising for cars, consumers said that word-of-mouth was the biggest influence 71% of the time.
> Source: Double Click Study

Tie that tidbit with the fact that over 80% of the decision makers for consumer products are female, add their propensity to gossip, and you have a marketing machine that can't be controlled. Your only defense in their access-to-all-knowledge world is to first provide an offering that will literally sell itself and then to become a master in what all women trust: the women's culture.

Selling itself is also referred to as "Organic" word-of-mouth. Many companies are trying to push Organic word-of-mouth by using "Amplified" word-of-mouth methods. You've seen them: cute jokes, funny videos,

3 ❧ Women: The Mega Market with the Megaphone

product placement, and now even paid people on the street talking up a product. All of these are designed to push along the good word on a product or service. But all of them will backfire if the product isn't worth its weight in gab. Women won't promote something to their friends, if they don't completely believe in it. They aren't about to risk their personal reputation or waste a friend's money on something they can't trust thoroughly.

> When a customer sees an ad, she knows it is an ad, and an increasing number of customers are tuning ads out. PR has a better chance of getting a message through.
> Source: Philip Kotler, Prof. Int'l Mktg, NWU

As the survey in Chapter One indicated, the majority of women trusted their gender first when it came to a service offering. While that "trust" happened long before the offering was defined, it is wrong to assume it just "happened." The inherent trust women have with one another is a product of both biological and social convergences which we'll explore in the next chapter.

With awareness comes understanding.

4 In Women We Trust, to Show Us *Their* Way

Trust is at an all-time low as indicated by the Trust Barometer Report from Edelman, the world's largest independent public relations firm. The Trust Barometer measures the attitudes of 1500 global leaders to determine who or what people trust. In 2005 only 24% of those interviewed felt they could trust the information on websites. CEOs fared worse at an 18% trust level. Paid advertisements – the most researched, art directed and strategically placed media to motivate a buyer's heart – came in at 10%! Yikes.

So what's the good news? We know what they are trusting – word-of-mouth. In 2003, the phrase "a person like yourself" garnered a 22% trust rating. Just two years later in 2005, the rating for "a person like yourself" went up to 56%.

The report isn't broken out by gender, but we can surmise that a "person like yourself" could mean a similar gender or culture. It then follows that women talking to other women will have the greatest impact on increasing or decreasing the trust factor.

The question most marketers are asking now is, "Who are these people that women trust and how can we get to them?" The bigger question to be answered is "Why did they (their friends) become *more trusted* than an offering or well crafted message?"

> *Why did their friends become more trusted?*

The answer is good old fashioned values, the kind that form deep friendships like respect, consideration, fun, safety, honesty, reliability, thoughtfulness… That's what made them friends in the first place and why they are trusted advisors now.

Do those values extend into business? Absolutely, that's why women are choosing their own culture first, *before* selecting a product with a heavy service component.

To look at it from a marketing perspective, it's the reverse of market segmentation where marketers segment their customers by age, home, financial condition, zip code, etc. This is more like "vendor value segmentation," where vendors are being segmented and selected by how many values they bring to the table that are just like their customer's values. It's not the surface personality the customers are buying, it's the integrity underneath.

We are more or less going back to the good old days when people did face-to-face business, which depended greatly on how the owner of the store treated the customer. If the town had one store, customers had no choice; but if the town had two stores, then who ran the store, how they

4   In Women We Trust, to Show Us *Their* Way

ran the store and what they did after the store closed, came into play. Customers would segment storeowners (or vendors) based on many things that often had nothing to do with the store contents. It's the original question: if all things were the same, who would you prefer to work with?

This isn't about offering gender-neutral products. If gender-neutral worked, women wouldn't be forming their own organizations all over the country duplicating the mixed-gender versions. They crave something else, something more like them.

> *They crave something else, something more like them.*

Now What Do We Do?

This gets especially confusing for women who have been schooled in corporate thinking and now are back in the small business world trying to relate to female customers on their terms. For example, a woman I know worked 21 years in a high corporate position for a Fortune 500 company. She left to start her own financial planning service and now she's having trouble shifting gears; the way her female clients operate is driving her nuts. Why? Because all those years in corporate taught her how to speak in bullet points and bottom-line terms. Meanwhile her female clients who weren't part of the corporate setting are talking, talking, talking.

"They are driving me crazy," she told me. "I'm used to people who can make fast decisions."

How does a business get past this? Can men learn another culture? For that matter, can women relearn their own? More importantly, can companies serving female consumers switch their corporate culture to one that carries more of their key customers' values?

> "Would you recommend us to a friend?"
> Fred Reichheld, author *Ultimate Question*

Sure, but it will take multiple exposures. Just like it takes more than one book, class, or tape before you're fluent in another language. Like any culture, each new generation will need training – no one is born proficient in their native tongue, they learn as they go. The best will be able to switch their mindsets between the traditional corporate way and the consumer way of doing things, based on which "relationship" they are in.

Keep the Brain, Change the Mindset

As in any step-by-step program (ours has nine), first you need to admit what you can't change. We understand that men can't change their brain patterns. To be honest, neither can women.

The "wiring in our brains" for thinking male or thinking female is loaded into our systems about 6-8 weeks after conception. During that time, the hormone that determines how male or female one becomes, gets dumped into the beginning cell mass, which eventually guides the development of the body from what sex it is, to *how that gender processes information.*

While you can't change what's given, understanding the differences can help keep both genders from thinking the other one is driving them crazy on purpose.

4 In Women We Trust, to Show Us *Their* Way

When it comes to "thinking," the male-developed brain tends to have activity take place in the left lobe (the predominately logical side). This is what keeps men laser focused on projects and able to tune out everything else.

The female brain, however, has activity happening on both sides, almost all the time. When men are resting, 30% of their brain remains active. When women are at rest, 90% remains active. Staying laser focused isn't our strong suit. Have you ever heard a woman say, "I can't seem to turn my brain off when I'm trying to sleep"? That's the problem, she really can't. All that between-the-lobes action is also what makes women great brainstormers during idea formation and great communicators when the idea needs to get passed along. It's probably why women feel comfortable in the field of marketing, a profession which requires both skills.

How men and women work online is also almost as different as night and day. A study by Resource Interactive and comSource Networks shows that very well. The researchers tracked 326,000 online purchases over the course of a year, watched how 50 men and women surfed sites, and surveyed 1000 more online participants. The net result mimicked what the offline world already tells us: the male gender processes things differently from the female gender. The male results lined up on the left hand side of the chart and the women's lined up on the right hand side. You could have drawn a line down the middle, it was that defined.

In one case, the men liked in-depth details and specifications and women preferred context in how the item will be used. Men took notes and women liked to visualize things. The only place they both agreed was preferring a feeling of "unity" over fragmentation. Ahhh, togetherness at last.

Just what are the women processing? Everything!

- Women have more cones in their eyes and therefore can see more colors.
- Women have greater peripheral vision – they literally take in the bigger picture.
- Their hearing is more acute.
- Their skin is 10 times more sensitive.
- Their taste buds are more discerning.
- Their sense of smell is heightened.

(If you want a fun and enlightening read into what makes both genders tick, buy a copy of *Why Men Don't Listen & Women Can't Read Maps,* by Barbara and Allan Pease.)

When people say, "women are more sensitive…" guess what – they are. They need that sensitivity to be better caretakers of children who can't say what's wrong. In an analysis of 125 studies on sensitivity, Northeastern University psychology professor, Judith Hall, PhD, determined that women generally surpassed men at decoding emotional messages.

It's also said that women are more intuitive – that's probably true as well. Considering that their entire sensory system takes in more information, they're bound to pick up additional nuances to guide their decisions.

4 In Women We Trust, to Show Us *Their* Way

What all this means is that women decide to "trust" a product, service, company or person based on thousands of seen and unseen information points, none of which have anything to do with the packaging, the presentation, or the brochure except when the personal risk is very low, such as when they're buying something as mundane as toothpicks.

It's "Personal," No Matter What They Say

Men say: "Don't take it personally, it's just business."

Women think (but would never say): "It *is* personal, or it's not business."

> Women think: "It *is* personal, or it's not business."

The cliché "don't take it personally, it's just business," makes perfect sense to a man who can compartmentalize. Men can also see business for what it is – just a game of wits – sometimes you win, and sometimes you lose. Products and services are simply an extension of that.

To a woman, however, business (products, services, people) will always be more personal. Three things bring me to that conclusion:

1. Because women sensually "experience" more, everything is more personal to them – the smell of the store, the loud music, waiting in line for eternity, the surly sales person… all that adds up to an overload of personal experience that men might not even notice.

This includes the personal time it takes to find, buy, and possibly return the item.

2. Women have a relationship style built on finding common ground (not one-upping each other, a trait often seen in the male culture). The common ground style is needed if they're going to be part of the group. One-upping puts them above the group. You can't "bond" if you act better than the rest; plus, no one likes a know-it-all.

3. "Reciprocal currency" is in a higher gear for women – call it the golden rule on estrogen. What women do for others, they expect back, more so than men do. Women have been socialized to work without pay for centuries: reciprocation has become their currency in an unseen barter network, where women help each other out. Since there is no money, they do the work for personal reasons. This is probably another reason that women do more volunteer work than men. They can feel the need and they are comfortable with the exchange rate.

> *"Reciprocal currency" – call it the golden rule on estrogen.*

In Women We Trust, to Show Us *Their* Way

Women are a generous lot. They would love it if companies focused only on them and served their needs well, but they are also wives and mothers who care deeply for their family and hope that they all get fair treatment. Consequently, women will tell you anything you want

4 ❖ In Women We Trust, to Show Us *Their* Way

to know to improve their world. All you have to do is ask – so we did.

At Interpret-her, the company of which I am a partner, we talked to a revolving panel of friends and professional women to comment on the upcoming chapter values. We didn't stop with one group, but used several intersecting circles of women. We also focused on midlife women as they are the first mass generation of women able to make economic choices for themselves. They also capture a lifetime of purchasing situations and the opinions that go with them. This was an unscientific survey meant to be a conversation starter.

In doing this we found that women trust women for many reasons. The first one is because they meet each other on common ground through their club, community, religious or business connections. That's not a cultural shift in their personal lives, but it is a cultural shift in how they conduct business.

Second, once women meet new people, they don't base their friendships on better price points. They choose friends based on whether they're **Respectful, Considerate, Fun, Safe, Honest, Reliable, Loyal,** or **Thoughtful** of others. There may be other ways to say it, but those values cover the gamut of trust points that make up a solid female friendship.

> Women don't base their friendships on better price points.

Companies or individuals who are struggling with the building or rebuilding of trust with their female customers (and maybe even their male customers) don't have to look much farther than how women value their friends. Hidden in those intangibles are the answers to formulating products, services, and messages that resonate with women instead of repelling them. This is both good and bad, when you open yourself up to *their truth* it may not be what you want to hear, but at least now you know.

We found that while it may take high marks in several of the values stated here to be considered a trusted "friend" behind the offering, messing up on just one value could also be grounds for dismissal.

For example, if your product is wonderful, but your sales staff is inconsiderate or disrespectful – women (more so than men) will walk. If the product or advice isn't safe, honest, and reliable... there will be no loyalty. And, since we are a global community, you'll leave us wondering if you are thoughtful enough to work towards the greater good or if you're just working toward being personally great?

All of the following values count – some more, some less – depending on the service or dollar value of the purchase. Use the questions at the end of each chapter to flesh out your own surveys.

Learn to earn her trust and become a part of the New Girls' Club.

Give women your trust and they'll give it back. Between what you think and what they tell you, you'll arrive at a closer idea of what women truly value in their business relationships. As a business you will learn how to earn her trust and become an integral part of the New Girls' Club.

5 The Community Spirit of Like-Minded Friends

Knowing why women are forming groups, inviting others to join, and then bonding with those they meet, is critical to understanding this culture shift.

I've been using the term 'group' when describing this dynamic, but a circle would be more accurate. Groups make you think of people huddled together for protection, that's not the case here. Women's communities are more like a round table where all are equal regardless of their skill level or connections. Rather than looking to a leader for direction, however, these women are looking to each other for guidance, inspiration and fun.

What Does "Community" Mean to You?

When we asked both men and women on our panel, "What does 'Community' mean to you?" each gender had very different answers.

The men gave short answers, such as, "My neighborhood, town, or condo complex," i.e., places where they lived. The women, however, responded with layers upon layers of communities. They included where they lived, then extended out to their kids' schools, their business buddies, religious groups, associations, college friends, garden clubs, book clubs, Internet discussion forums, and chat rooms. To them, communities were anywhere they parked their brains based on common needs, and included people they met in the process.

> Community is a group of people that I have a connection to because we have a sense of shared purpose or certain things in common... I look for friends [who] have similar values to mine.
> Public relations specialist, age 39

To be fair, when the men heard what the women said, they responded with their own additional groups, but the fact is, they didn't see the groups as a first-tier, gut-reaction item. They also didn't have as many groups on their final list as the women.

Not only do women have *more* communities, they relate differently to the subject matter within them. Let's take book clubs, for example. Judy B. Rosener, the author of *America's Competitive Secret – Women Managers*, decided to attend all-male and all-female book clubs to see if they differed. She observed that the men would talk about the book, but the women would talk about how the book *related to them*.

Another woman commented how her book club doesn't read books anymore. The club started out that way, but everyone so enjoyed each other's company that they stopped reading assigned books and now get together *just to talk*. It's the social interaction that keeps them coming back.

5 ❋ The Community Spirit of Like-Minded Friends

Group Dynamics at Work or Play

The social interactions of the book club attendees would be the same with almost any other women's group. You'd expect the same thing if you were changing churches: the group dynamics might be a little different, but the basic belief system is the same.

Rick Warren, the pastor of Saddleback Church in Orange County, California, and author of *The Purpose Driven Life,* understands the power of small groups. He managed to take a church of 250 people and turn it into a congregation of 20,000. At its core are small groups – all of them following a similar evangelical creed, which they are encouraged to explore in a multitude of ways. The dogma may be the same, but the way each group experiences it is completely up to them.

What Pastor Warren understands is that these small groups *are* the church. It doesn't matter if they are biking, bowling or sharing a book; it's the interaction among those 10 or so people that forms the bond and the foundation of the greater group.

Women's groups take a similar path. The greater connection *per se* is the "women's way" of doing things and the small groups reinforce those shared values. How they behave inside the small group is really a reflection of their collective whole. These small groups *are* the women's culture.

> You're known in your community – or else you aren't really part of it.
> Cable TV program director, age 52

The women's way isn't country-specific; it's a universal method of interconnected support. In India, through a micro-lending system, women can start their own business with just $50 or $100. They join a group of 8-10 other women who support each other during their individual start-up process. If one woman can't pay back the loan because of family hardship or some other unforeseen force, the other women help to pay it back for her. Consequently, the default percentage for these loans is under 5% – less than any traditional business loan in the U.S. Communal support and trust among friends is what makes it work.

At a recent meeting for the National Association of Women Business Owners (NAWBO) in Orange County, CA, that same support exhibited itself. One woman was able to take her business from $1 million to $2 million in one year because of the help she received from the women in her NAWBO group.

The "New Girls' Club"

Regardless of what brings women together, "The New Girls' Club" lets women be themselves – to laugh and work without feeling self-conscious. This is where they can tell their stories and get positive feedback. It's also where they can ask questions without fear of feeling dumb and where they practice their leadership skills, over and over.

> I expect things from the people in my personal community like loyalty, support, and friendship and I give the same things back.
> Web manager, age 45

The "New Girls' Clubs" don't have walls or outrageous initiation fees to keep people out, but in a way, they are harder to get "inside." As a business, you can buy

5   The Community Spirit of Like-Minded Friends

awareness via sponsorships and ads, but only full interaction on their level will make you one of the girls in these clubs.

Where Business and Female Communities Connect

How does a company become a member of a women's community? By behaving as it would if it was a member of the community, which includes having the same values that the women cherish in each other.

As a member, how others see you in the group is completely dependant on your personality. What you put into the group with a spirit of openness and sincerity is what you'll get back. The closer you can get to friendship-based business, the less baggage either you or the customer has to deal with. When female customers know that you truly care and are trying to help them, they overlook a lot of growing pains and goof ups. That's reciprocal currency in action and it doesn't matter if the community is online or offline.

Adding money to the mix doesn't negate the above, it only ups the ante. Just because women are paying for something, doesn't mean you can overlook the friendship values of her culture. The women in Chapter One's survey trusted other women first because they felt that women offered more personal value to the contracted service.

> Less malpractice lawsuits happen to doctors who take an extra few minutes to be friendly with their patients.
> Source: Berkeley Rice, Medical Economics, July 11, 2003

Female Employees:
Community Building from the Inside, Out

Are your female employees jazzed about your company and its offerings enough to spread the word? If they aren't, then getting customers to get jazzed and spread the word will be even harder.

In the documentary "The Corporation," (found at www.thecorporation.com), the filmmakers examined corporations as if they were individuals to be praised or sued accordingly. They took corporations-at-large and profiled their personalities based on the same things people normally use to rate individuals. For instance, were the corporations gracious and generous to others, or did they lie, steal or kill? Sadly, the conclusion was that many corporations are "psychotic," and if they were actual individuals, they would probably need to seek legal or psychiatric help. Certainly that isn't true of all corporations, but it does give one pause to see it in that perspective.

What about your product, service, or company: are you prepared for a word-of-mouth world? Are you viewed as psychotic, depressed or confident? Trust your female employees, they'll tell you. You might have to use a third party to get to the truth, but your employees will tell you, if you approach them properly.

> Community is everything which makes up one's personal world. It can be an international thing or in one's daily life.
> Corporate relations manager, 42

Even if you aren't going to launch a word-of-mouth campaign, an in-house review with your female employees is worth conducting. Female employees not

5 ✺ The Community Spirit of Like-Minded Friends

only represent the gender you're trying to understand, but they'll give more details as to why something works or doesn't.

The Internet makes even the smallest companies "transparent." Public records are out there for everyone to see, and if they aren't readily available, customers and employees can write about the company on blogs, in chat rooms, or on bulletin boards. Because of that, the company's "public sum total" spreads as good or bad word-of-mouth. Working with your female employees could flag problems before they get out of hand.

Your internal female community is yours to tap. Embrace the fact that you'll get the negative with the positive, and also that many employees will be outside of your typical demographic. They may not need the service themselves, but you can bet they know someone who does. It's better to learn their thoughts, away from the lights of public opinion, than to find out later on from some disgruntled blogger who can wreck your reputation in one posting – and may do so anonymously!

> If I'm not on the same page with those around me and I find myself doing most of the support work, I tend to withdraw and will eventually find a new community that feels more in sync value-wise. I've let friends go, separated from organizations, switched jobs and moved homes under this circumstance.
>
> Print media manager, age 38

Would They Recommend You?

By asking female employees their opinion of your company, you accomplish several things. First, you empower them with a voice which normally isn't heard at a high enough level. Second, if the information is applied, they can see that their opinions are directly affecting change. Lastly, the process starts a conversation buzz among the female employees that the company really does care about them (as people), and also cares about the greater good.

Wow. Look at that, you just built your own female community – women helping women stay employed by putting out better products or services. Now there's a cause we'll all want to join.

> I'm very, very loyal if I feel that the community is supportive, friendly, comfortable, non-judgmental/accepting, genuine/authentic and works for all involved.
>
> Corporate manager, 47

Turning Customers into Your Community

Is your offering so unique that it naturally fills a niche like no other – enough to create its own following like ipod?

To find out, take what you learned from your female employees, fine-tune it and now talk to your female customers. Give them the same air time and attention that you gave your staff and add their answers to the mix.

After you learn what they feel is important on a "base value level," you have the basis for a good word-of-mouth campaign. If you look at a women's incoming email box of forwards from friends, most items are either "fun," "educational" or "inspirational." To spread your word-of-mouth campaign among women, try to work your offering into one of those areas.

5 The Community Spirit of Like-Minded Friends

Leveraging External Communities

Once you know your strengths, you're ready to match them with some pre-existing women's groups. This is Marketing 101 thinking: find your "target" and go for it – but with caution. Remember, you cannot "buy" word-of-mouth, you can only finesse it. If your goal is to build a reputation worthy of chatter, then you must always test your own sincerity of purpose, and allow others to push it forward or not.

Think what would happen if you were a guy attending a women's group. You're already "not-one-of-them," but instead of waiting to be introduced into the group, you hand a business card to everyone you meet. This might be an accepted practice at a mixed-gender networking group, but not in a women's group. It's too pushy, and no one wants to be someone's "target."

> We have to be careful with who we let sponsor an event; we don't want to appear like we're endorsing a product that isn't beneficial to our patients.
>
> Hospital administrator of consumer affairs, age 45

As the trust factor in traditional advertising continues to erode, marketing to women through their networks will increase. If it isn't a good match and done with sincerity, it will be labeled for what it is (a tactic) – and dismissed. On the other hand, if you meet people casually, show a sincere interest in their lives, and become an active resource for them, you will eventually get recommended. With the Internet, it's no longer a slow way to build a business. Ongoing referrals are free, so why not? Besides, word will spread – with your help or not – so why not become part of the generating mechanism?

Are you consistent?

Test, test, test yourself for corporate personality consistency. Women may love or hate Howard Stern because they know what they are getting. Women may love or hate Ben & Jerry's ice cream because they know what they are getting there as well. What they can't handle in a small community (or an interconnected one) is inconsistency. Inconsistency makes women feel like the rat pushing a bar to get food one minute but getting a shock the next. They can plan ahead for either, but when both happen, they don't know what to do. Women just don't have time to do research over and over. If they have a choice, they'll go with the product or service that is the most consistent.

The ChitChat business model

Tupperware became a billion dollar industry and set the foundation for the chitchat business model by being consistent and leveraging women's natural communities. The product had to be useful to one woman, however, before she would recommend it to others. Moreover, if it didn't keep working for years, that one woman would not have continued to represent it. After all, she was selling it to neighbors and friends, and her personal reputation was on the line.

Millions of women working from their homes keep Tupperware sales going. No one is keeping men from holding parties, yet only a handful of them do. Why? The chitchat model isn't a natural part of the way men communicate. That said, if women can learn how to fit

5 ✺ The Community Spirit of Like-Minded Friends

into a corporate setting, then men can learn how to fit into a consumer setting by appreciating how communities work for women.

✺ Check Your Community Trust Points…

Where do you have common ground?

Where can you be reciprocal?

What have you done for their community that would make them want to recommend you?

1. Which communities do your customers interact with on a regular basis (offline and online)? Which communities do your female employees interact with?
2. What are the topics that brought the women to their community? (gardening, religion, environment)
3. Can you identify the top ten topics that pull women in?
4. Which groups have the greatest following?
5. Which groups do they stay with the longest? Why?
6. What do they "get" from being with the group? (Education, friendship, leadership opportunities)

7. Which of their communities does your company currently intersect with?

8. Do you have an ongoing education program that can be offered into their communities? Is it *pro bono*?

9. If a woman or her community brings you business, do you have a way of rewarding her/it for thinking about you?

10. Can one woman tell another woman about your company in one sentence? What would it be?

6 Respectful of Her Background and Ideas

This is where trust starts; without an inherent respect for your women customers and clients, everything else falls a little short. Having respect is a mindset, you either see women as equal partners in the buyer/seller equation or you don't. Do you consider them fully functioning human beings that have their own values worth honoring or not? The sales, marketing, or advertising that happens next, emanates from that point of view.

Women give other women more respect because they are "just like them." Their experiential base may be drastically different as far as home or work life, but their common ground – the female experience – unites them. Midlife women especially know how hard it was/is to "get the job," "keep the job, "raise the kids," "clean the house," "be perfect," *etc*… They don't have to explain

> When visiting a person in a different culture, you "respect" or acknowledge their cultural rules – the foods they eat, their religious rites, the 'garments' they wear.
>
> Realtor, age 52

themselves in front of other women; that common knowledge is shared without a word being said.

Common Experience – The Big Dismissal

One of the unspoken common experiences is feeling dismissed or invisible based on nothing more than being female. It happens inside a family, in business, and even in public depending on your ethnic group.

We took an informal survey of 50 adults which was made up of about half men and half women, from different age groups. We were hoping to gather sage advice to present at an upcoming birthday party. The question was, *"What do you know now that you wished you knew at 18?"*

We expected to see similar answers based on age. What emerged, however, was a division between what men wished they had known and what women wished to do over.

With the exception of a few men, the men wished that they had known more about managing their careers and their money – saving it, investing it, staying away from credit cards, *etc*.

Most of the married women wished that they had finished getting their college degrees, postponed marriage, or, if married, had put off having kids – in short, they wished they had a life of their own before they gave their lives over to a family. Whether or not they would admit it publicly, they viewed marriage and family as the end of their learning/exploring days – at least until the kids

6 ❊ Respectful of Her Background and Ideas

were launched. Single women for the most part also wished they had put more effort into their education and traveled more.

This echoes a study conducted in Australia in response to the marriage and birth rate decline. Having access to birth control was certainly a contributor, but what they also found was that women saw themselves as second class citizens once they became mothers. They noted how they "disappeared" in importance upon having children. That message was permeating the female culture and consequently, more Australian women were opting to remain in the "first class," i.e.: childless.

> I would have gone to college. Did what my heart told me to do rather than what society expected me to do.
> Print director, age 54

This theme showed up again, on the other end of raising kids, in a survey taken by Jane Glenn Haas the founder of WomanSage. The survey posted on www.WomanSage.com received responses from over 3000 midlife women. Since WomanSage addresses the needs of this population, the survey wanted to know: "How is your life different from your mother's?" The results? Besides being more in control than their mothers, they also felt that it was "their turn now." This age group had balanced motherhood and careers and was now ready to focus on lives of their own.

Notice that none of the above examples has anything to do with a typical demographic market segment. All of them have to do with the roles women play in society, and how those roles dismissed them to the back of the class, and continue to do so, even now. It's no wonder women are turning to cultures "just like them," where they feel good and are respected for the contributions they've made and continue to make. No one wants to feel bad about her life's work.

How Do Female Friends Show Each Other Respect?

The panel gave us pages of opinions as to how they know when they are receiving "respect," or not receiving it. It came down to four topics, the women felt that their friends were showing them respect when:

- *They respected their intelligence.* Friends would talk with them, not at them or down to them. They took the time to know them. Their friends understood the difference between being silly or being stupid, and were able to roll with it.

- *They respected and acknowledged their accomplishments at home and at work*; first by taking the time to find out what those accomplishments were and then acknowledging the work they did.

- *They respected their life choices and didn't judge them or criticize them*. By not putting a damper on their process, the friends allowed other women to develop their own path as fast or as slow as they liked.

- *They respected their time.* Friends helped them save time by helping them with tasks or simply by not making them wait.

Sometimes the women found it easier to define respect by *when it was missing* rather than what was apparent.

6 ❧ Respectful of Her Background and Ideas

For example, one woman said, "They treated me like a two-year-old," instead of saying, "They treated me like a goddess." Many women, when they were answering that question, noted where respect was missing first. That's good news for companies: it means there is room for improvement. If companies can help women feel the positive aspects of respect first, it will position them ahead of those who do nothing.

Respecting Intelligence

Women communicate with a lot of other smart women on a daily basis. It's not only invigorating; it helps to add to each other's knowledge base. Midlife women have been growing older with the same group of women making up the list of the movers and shakers in Chapter Two. They know that there is a good chance the women they meet either have a college degree or most certainly have life experiences that are just as valuable as theirs. Also, in the midlife group their defenses are down. They've either "made it" or not and it doesn't matter anyway – at this point everyone has had some success or failure in her life; it's what makes us all the same.

Why should you care? Because more times than not, women get labeled the moment they walk into a store or office. It's understandable. It's easy to treat someone like "Mom" if you're 23 and someone your mom's age walks in. It's human nature to attach the same characteristics to someone new based on people you already know. In the same way, if a younger woman comes

> When someone treats me as though I'm at least their equal, I feel they're being respectful.
> Corporate manager, age 61

57

in, she might be put in the "sister" column. The truth is – both should go into one column–the knowledgeable customer column.

> People who respect me don't talk down to me. They listen and discuss, and don't discount my feelings or thoughts.
> — Dental hygienist age 52

Midlife women have been shopping their whole lives. They probably have purchased and furnished three homes and put millions of miles on at least eight cars, not to mention decades of managing a career, home and multiple roles. They are self-taught in the fine art of comparison shopping.

Today, you can expect them to augment that schooling with Internet research. As a paying customer, "Mom" definitely knows more than you and for that matter, even a 20-year-old woman knows more than you–she knows what she wants, and you don't.

By building on what your women customers know at 20 or 50, you respect their intelligence and experience. Start from where they are, not where you think they should be or where they should end up. Don't short-cut the steps just to close the sale faster. Go at their speed.

> As I've aged, I'm more sensitive to being respected and less willing to put up with being disrespected – especially in business.
> — Geologist, age 53

Respecting Accomplishment at Home and at Work

I was at a conference last year when one of the speakers asked the audience of healthcare executives, "How many of you get too much recognition?" Everyone in the room laughed, but no one raised a hand. Even if they did receive lots of recognition, there is no such thing as too much.

Countless articles in countless magazines restate this overriding issue—women feel underacknowledged. But they can often gain back acknowledgement from being part of a women's group. Women do a great job of giving each other spontaneous gifts of encouragement and rewards, "just because." They ask each other about work or the family and then they listen for how the day really went. They recognize the person first and then what they are doing, as well.

Maybe that's why volunteer organizations run by women work the same way. They acknowledge the person first and then the contribution. It's using social currency to its best advantage, where everyone wins.

In 2005, 100 top women in Orange County, CA were honored for their contributions to business and the community.

> Respect to me is synonymous with acknowledgement.
> Student, age 35

The women were selected for producing top ranked magazines, running nationwide organizations or re-organizing hundreds of restaurants until they started making a profit, etc. You get the picture.

There wasn't a slacker among them and all were highly successful by any monetary standard of management, yet monetary gain was conspicuous by its absence. Instead, heard among the accolades were stories of how they met every employee, talked with customers, cajoled city leaders, or motivated families. The successes they achieved were accomplished through personal connections much the same as if these women were running a volunteer organization. They were successful because of their personal approach and their respect for those working with them, employees and customers, alike.

> Having respect has a lot to do with being well-mannered.
> Research analyst, age 48

Respecting Their Choices Without Judgment

Everyday we make choices. For women, it's important that their choices are seen as just as valid as anyone else. Women tend to be less judgmental of other women's choices since we're all just "learning the ropes" together – different ropes maybe, but all still learning.

This statement, by a woman, was overheard at a woman's event, "My family would think I'm crazy for changing jobs at this point in my life." To which another women in the group responded, "That's why you're here, for the support you need."

Jodi Foster, Hollywood actor and director of many motion pictures, commented in an NPR interview that, "Women in Hollywood get one chance to do good work, where men are given chance upon chance."

That mentality of "one chance and you're out" is what keeps some women from giving real answers during mixed-gender conversations. It isn't that they don't have an opinion; it's just that their opinion has one chance to be perfect, and they would rather not take that chance so they keep it to themselves. How do you offset that? Just keep asking sincere questions until she trusts you enough to give you answers.

Respecting Her Time

Time is the mother lode of the respect issue. We got an earful on this one, but we'll let the facts speak first:

- Women do 60% of the caretaking for elderly parents.
- Women are making decisions on 80% of the consumer products and services.
- They manage the health care for their households.
- They perform 60% of the housework.
- They do the majority of volunteer work.

It all adds up to, "Eeeeeeek, what happened to my weeeeeek!"

Source:
What Women Really Want: How American Women are Quietly Erasing, Political, Racial, Class, and Religions Lines to Change the Way We Live Forever by Celinda lake, Kellyanne Conway, Catherine Whitney (FreePress, 2005)

Save Her Time

Saving her time is a nicety that women extend to other women and if a product or service can do it as well, you're on your way to bonding.

Women, especially moms, have to balance every minute against the to-do list. Because of that, they are also very sensitive about how they "spend" other people's time, and would appreciate it in return.

A few months back, my neighbor called me in a panic, "Could you come down and stay with the baby while I go to the hospital?" (Her older daughter had broken her arm while skateboarding.) She met me at her door with snacks for the baby, then in the middle of her frantic need to leave she stopped and asked, "Is this okay? Do you have time to do this?" Rather than focusing completely on her crisis, she took a moment to respect my time commitment.

> Others may make more money, but all of us have the same amount of currency in time.
> Dental hygienist, age 51

Be On Time, Her Friends Do That

Women handle 65% of the car repairs and, sadly, 85% of us are not happy with the experience. Waiting for anyone after scheduling an appointment is irritating, but think about what a mother goes through. First she has to find a babysitter or load up the kids, then drive through traffic or snow, or both. It doesn't really matter what she had to go through to get to the appointment, the point is she went through it and now she's waiting *for someone to walk across a room to keep their half of the appointment.* What happens? She continues to wait. That's a heck of a way to treat a friend who isn't paying you -and unforgivable to do to a customer who is.

Home repair services are just as bad. Can you imagine how long you'd remain friends if someone said, "I'll be over on Thursday, sometime between 7 a.m. and 7 p.m. – just take the day off of work and I'll be there when I can." Women wouldn't ask that of their friends, so why

6 ❦ Respectful of Her Background and Ideas

do companies ask it of women (and men) who they'd like to keep as customers?

The converse is also true – when an appointment is made, but ignored – and happens on a business-to-business level, as well. A female friend of ours works at a local college and was in charge of finding architects to design a new building. She put the job out to bid and went with a group that offered the best ideas for a reasonable fee. No sooner had they secured the bid then they started showing up late for meetings, first 30 minutes, then an hour. These were meetings that they, the architects, had scheduled.

> If my time is not considered important, then I'm going to end up angry, irritated and a customer no more.
> Lawyer, age 55

One day, she decided not to wait. She and her staff met for the 2:00 meeting, went over the construction details of the day and were wrapping up the meeting when the architects finally arrived.

They were stunned that she would meet without them. She was stunned that they would bid a job and consistently miss their own meetings. She was polite to them, but very angry at their lack of respect for her staff's time. Their work was good, but their lack of respect cost them future contracts and a referral.

What about Returning Phone Calls?

How long would you remain friends if you left a message and your friend took a day or two before calling back? That's typically what happens when anyone uses email at a customer service site.

Women don't accept those conditions from a friend, not for long anyway, nor do we accept them from a face-to-face encounter at a store. Why then do website owners think that getting back to a customer a day or two later is good enough? To women, who spend the majority of their time interacting – on the phone, email, or in person – it seems very disrespectful of their time (and culture) and it's a quick way to lose a sale before it starts.

When Time Means More than Money

Younger women value their time just as much as their midlife friends. A GenY member in her 20s gave us an example of how she was given a $75 gift certificate to her favorite clothing store. To this day, the certificate remains uncashed. This young woman reported that the place was such a mess that even though she was in the store with free money (money that couldn't be spent anywhere else), it still wasn't worth her time. The sloppy presentation was like being invited to a home that hasn't been cleaned in months. It's not very hospitable and you wouldn't do it to a friend, but this store felt it was okay to do it to their customers.

Forget Double Coupons, Give Her Double Time

Here are a few ideas that are both respectful and practical to help her expand her time:

- Quick Med X, a new service which employs nurse practitioners for small aches and pains, operates in Target, CVS and Cub Stores. **Some stores give patients a beeper so they can shop the superstore while waiting their turn.**

- If you have complex services, first make your website incredibly easy to navigate and keep it "clean." Don't overload it with information that can lead her away from her goal; **give her context and more visuals than specifications – and free shipping helps.** She's there to get her research or shopping done and onto the next project. Making it easy for her to shop at home is the ultimate way to double her time.

- **Give her a toll free number on the front page of your website**. Nothing says, "We don't want to talk to you" like making her dig through contact pages to get your number and then discovering a number that isn't toll free. A friend would say, "Call me anytime, day or night." Will you do the same? Let her do research AND talk to a professional.

- While you're at it, **provide several different communication choices**; phone, email, instant messaging, Voice over Internet – give her options to make quicker connections.

- Set up a system that lets the SAME person work with a customer until the order has been placed or the problem solved. As a society, we understand job turnover, but **customer service turnover from one minute to the next is frustrating and wastes time re-telling the story again and again.**

- If she is in your physical store or business, **give her what she needs to stay on task, i.e. a place for her kids to hang out, quiet areas to think**, and above all a sociable and knowledgeable staff that can really help her through the pros and cons of her final decision.

- **Provide services while she is at work.** In California, a car cleaning service travels from office complex to complex cleaning, washing and waxing cars while owners work.

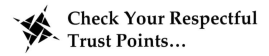
Check Your Respectful Trust Points...

Where do you have common ground?

Where can you be reciprocal?

How do customers know that you're respectful of women in general?

1. Do your female employees feel like they have your company's respect?

2. If your hiring policies were made public, would the market agree that your employees are respected?

3. Do you have cultural training in place to help your sales and service team become more

6 — Respectful of Her Background and Ideas

empathetic to a woman's life experience? (Women need it too!)

4. Do you visually acknowledge what her lifestyle brings to your business (offline and online)?

5. Do you encourage your staff to be inclusive, to make sure they have an even exchange of information with a customer, instead of simply telling them what to do?

6. If you put your company through time trials for answering the phone, email, mail, website… how would you score?

7. Do you have a LIVE person answering questions for both sales and service?

8. Do you have an active "time-savers" program to make her buying job easier? Hint: it isn't a time saver if it's fast for you, but confuses her.

9. What have you *done* that indicates your company has respect for women? How would they know, even if they never saw your advertising?

10. Does your management embody a respectful stance that permeates through your company? This is more than being politically correct–we are talking about the kind of change where respect "training" isn't needed. It's part of the corporate culture.

7 Considerate of Her Needs

Are you considerate?

Of course you are. We all like to think of ourselves as considerate individuals. We also like to think that we're respectful, fun, safe, honest, reliable, loyal and thoughtful. So what's the problem? If companies are made up of nothing but nice people, then why do service complaints show up on the consumer opinion sites?

One reason, may be lack of education.

First of all, some employees may not know what being considerate means – from a women's perspective. Second, if they do know, maybe company policy prevents consideration from happening. Third, three people in the company could be doing everything right, while a fourth person blows it. That fourth person could be the salesperson who didn't return a call or it could be the curt receptionist. All the customer remembers is that the last person (or the first one) that she had contact with wasn't considerate. That person's action now defines the whole company.

One of our panelists related a classic story. She had flown into Los Angeles with her 9-year-old daughter and rented a car at 1 a.m. A few minutes later a city truck backed into the rental car, forcing her to return the car at 2 a.m. She's tired, her kid's tired and yet, when she asked the rental car staff for assistance, the response was, "I have to fill the stapler first." She was stunned. She said to us, "Do you think I have ever rented from that car agency again?"

So what's the big deal? Sometimes you win, sometimes you lose, right?

That cavalier attitude worked when you had an ever-expanding crowd of customers who never talked to one another. Today, with email, chat rooms and unlimited phone service, it's time to tighten up the loose ends before they become lost customers.

What's the "Considerate" Common Ground for Women?

Once again, the women on our panel contributed pages of thoughts that came down to a few trust points:

- Be a good listener (take them seriously, acknowledge their thoughts and feelings).
- Have patience (they are thinking out loud and many things are new).
- Put others' needs and feelings ahead of your own (like they do).
- Say "thank you" (it's a BIG part of their culture).

- Stay in touch (to show you really care).

Is this common ground for both genders? Let's test it. Say the same statements again, only this time imagine the words coming from a male CEO: *"Be a good listener, acknowledge women's thoughts or feelings, put their needs ahead of your own, say thank you, and stay in touch."*

"Being considerate" isn't how wars are won or corporate battles fought. This is why they don't ring true for the corporate culture in general - a model based on top-down, military and industrial structure that refers to customers as a "target market." Say the words again, only this time imagine them coming from a female CEO. Do they seem more feasible even though she's part of the same corporate culture as the male CEO?

Therein lays the challenge for those trying to align themselves with female customers. Forget what is "considerate" inside the corporation: can your offerings be "considerate" on a woman's terms? Are you willing to alter your corporate mindset to match her ideal?

Two-way Conversations, the Beginning of a Sale

If there is one thing that women do well, it's making conversation. Consequently, if there is one thing on the top of their wish list, it's to be a good listener. They talk and listen all day long as part of their regular communications and they expect the same "consideration" in all relations, both business and personal.

Companies would be better off teaching their sales and marketing departments the art of hosting - how to encourage conversations and create atmospheres of inclusion - rather than how to give a "pitch" on features and benefits. Pitches are "just business." Winning customers over is personal.

> Being considerate is making the other feel comfortable during any kind of interaction.
> Artist, age 56

To have a "meaningful" conversation with your female customer requires just two things:

1. Take her seriously.
2. Acknowledge that what she says carries weight with you.

Can you listen and respond as if it was the first time hearing a problem like hers? Are you open to more information? Can you converse like that whether it's in person, on the phone, on the web, or on a blog? Can you be a sounding board without sounding bored?

Women need to think out loud and other women know and accept this. Rarely do they tell another woman to cut to the bottom line. That would be rude. While thinking out loud and explaining the problem, they often come up with their own answer. What do they say, then? "Thanks, I guess I just needed to talk about it."

Being an excellent sounding board helps that process. For those not accustomed to the fine art of active listening, it isn't "parroting," or repeating what you just heard. That's annoying to most and shows that you really weren't listening in the first place. Try this instead:

1. Ask a woman a question and listen for what is being said (ponder it).

7 ❊ Considerate of Her Needs

2. Ask a second question to get clarification on a point of view or information just given (ponder it for another moment).
3. Ask a third question to get an even deeper level of understanding.

What will happen?

First, she'll be *delighted* that you asked. It's always flattering to be asked your opinion and because it's rare, even in this era of equality, it stands out. It means that on some level, she is seen as an authority or that her opinion matters (and therefore she matters).

Second, she'll be *charmed* that you really heard what she was saying and you took it seriously enough to want to know specifics. Don't launch into a sales pitch based on the answer to the first question. Take time to get to know her and her needs better. Good hosting comes first; besides, you can't help her until you're both working to resolve the same problem.

> Consideration to me means looking at a situation from my perspective and really understanding my wants and needs.
> — Lawyer, age 51

Third, she'll be *stunned* by your intelligence and your ability to process information.

Okay, that's a flippant summary, but by asking a third question, you confirmed your sincerity of purpose: *helping her is all that matters.*

After three questions, most women ask a question back and the conversation begins. Congratulations, you just made yourself into a sounding board that can help her make an "informed" decision.

By asking at least three questions you are automatically doing something else - you are acknowledging that what she said is being "taken into consideration." By "pondering" what is said, you give more weight to *her thoughts and/or feelings* on the topic. This is a "tactic" only until it becomes natural and then it becomes what it should be: good give-and-take conversation where both parties are equal in power and importance. It also slows you down so you aren't rushing to make *your* next selling point. Rushing means you're not listening.

Have you ever been frustrated while talking to someone who answers your statement with, "That's not true..."? And, before you can respond, they provide the truth as they know it? This is where most sales conversations with women go south. While a man might battle back with a different view or tactic, women often let the conversation die, rather than get into what they perceive as a confrontation. While you're busy making your point, your partner in conversation is thinking you didn't take what she said seriously, so why bother to continue?

While letting women talk increases the sales cycle, is it a waste of time? Never. The more they talk, the more you learn about them and about serving the entire gender better. They are also investing time in you and for that reason they'll be more open to your comments when it comes time for you to talk. The best guideline is to give them options and help them refine their decision, but never make the decision for them.

Be Patient

Statistics show that about 47% of women over 40 are single. The other 53% are married and often have an entire family to consider in their decision making. Those women need lots of information to know how your offering will work for the whole group. Questions that provide *context* as to how it will be used for all age groups are more useful during this stage. Until she can articulate how the offering will be used, she can't look for the best solution.

While you're helping women, you're also making friends. Your female customers may not need the service again for a long time, as in the case of buying a car. However, they will gladly tell their friends how delightful it was to work with someone who actually listened and understood how their needs matter.

Women: Putting Others First

I don't think I'll get an argument if I say that women consistently put the needs of others ahead of themselves. It's almost a rite of womanhood. Consequently, when a business puts *her* first, it gets noticed on a very basic level.

How does this apply to business? Here's a great example. A friend who was a longtime owner of Hondas went shopping for a new Acura. At Lot #1, she approached the male salesperson and said, "I want a 6-cylinder with a sun roof and I want it in red or black." He took her to a white car with no sun roof, then to a 4-cylinder car. She told him that wasn't what she wanted, and left to go to another lot.

At Lot #2, the same thing happened. She gave her exact requirements and the salesperson led her to cars that didn't fill any of them. She left and went to a third lot.

Lot #3 also didn't have anything available, but the male salesperson did have a connection to the Internet. He went online to find the exact match at another Lot and offered to bring it to theirs. Salesperson #3 listened, took this woman's needs seriously, found what she wanted, and she bought the car from him.

> Responsiveness and follow-through are key for me. When I'm in a situation where I'm being treated with a high degree of both, on a consistent basis, I feel understood, important and valued.
>
> Corporate manager, age 42

How simple can a sale be? That simple! Salesperson #3 put this woman's needs ahead of clearing out personal inventory. He not only made the sale, he also gained a new service customer. It wouldn't matter if the sales person was male or female; the point is, Lot #3 put her first (the same way she puts others first) and that is a cultural difference, not a gender difference.

The Queens of "Thank you"

Telling someone "Thanks" is almost a lost art in the business world. When you thank customers, are you really giving it a sincere effort or just automating the process?

If you're automating it, you might as well not do anything. Women are schooled, either directly by their mothers or indirectly by social dictates, to send personal cards and thank you notes. Since they do it for others, they expect and appreciate it when others do it for them. Even though busy lives are forcing women to cut back on written correspondence, it doesn't mean they have forgotten it, or that they won't appreciate a sincerely written note.

Once, while I was waiting for my car to be repaired, I noticed a bulletin board full of letters. Nine out of eleven were handwritten thank you cards from women. Two typed letters on company stationery were from men. I wasn't surprised. Men may be as thankful as women but women express it more often and more personally.

The irony here is that the bulletin board represents customers thanking a business for doing a job which they paid to have done! I wonder if that same business reciprocated by calling each of them and at least acknowledging their letters.

How about in person? Are women more thankful? Yes. How often have you heard a man say, "Thank you *SO* much!" I can name one guy and about 12 women, just off the top of my head. Nothing says "I recognize what you have done for me" like a heartfelt thanks.

When Women Say, "Stay in touch," They Mean It

Female friends stay in touch through phone calls, email, birthdays, and holidays. Staying in touch means just that, in-*touch* not in-*mass-mailing*. "In touch" means talking, interacting, checking on the person during times when business isn't necessary. This is where actions really do speak louder than words.

When a woman is sick or going through a tough transition (like divorce or losing a job), her friends know it immediately and help her over the bumps in life's road. Why? Because when they were going through their own transitions, she was there for them. It's reciprocal currency being honored and exchanged. It's women being women, where giving is a part of what they do.

Staying in touch is part of "giving." Not all offerings need this sort of hands-on attention, but the ones involving professional one-to-one services certainly do. Through the years, one of our panel members had five financial planners - four men and one woman. Not once did any of the men call her during the year; not even for a year end check-up. Now she has a female planner who stays in touch and responds to every email or phone call - usually within 2 hours. Plus, she's taken a personal interest in this woman's life. That personal interest is something our panel member sees as important. If something happens to her, the financial planner needs to know how to work with her husband as well. Would a man do the same? So far, the four men she's worked with have taught her that they won't.

Maybe this is purely gender related. I recently read a blog on "How to get better service from your financial planner." According to the male writer, the customer needs to keep in touch with the planner and thank them for the service they contracted to provide. Perhaps that's why the women in the example above didn't get a call from her male planners: in the men's minds they thought it was the customer's duty to stay in contact. From female perspective, she felt it was their duty to initiate regular contact. The male planners were doing what men do - leave you alone until you want something. She was thinking what women think: "What's wrong? Why don't they call? Don't they care?"

Staying in touch between business moments sends a strong message that the person matters in a way that's more than "just business." It also allows the professional to know a client's "life story" so they can make better personal, financial, medical or legal decisions on the client's behalf when a critical moment does come along.

If you were a women, who would you want working for you? Someone who has taken the time to know your life story? Or one who manages problems as the problems happen, with no context for providing advice? The first is "personal;" the second "efficient," but not necessarily effective. Since we've shown that women aren't forthcoming with information if they don't feel comfortable, then meeting them only during business hours won't improve their candor.

That said, there is a point where good intentions become annoying even for women. Women are busy; a lunch meeting or a personal check-in call once a quarter is appreciated, if she's already a client. Calling more than once a quarter just to sell her something is irritating. It's better to build the relationship through a common community instead.

Check Your Considerate Trust Points…

Where do you have common ground?

Where can you be reciprocal?

Do your female customers feel that you have been considerate of them in person and long distance via the web or telephone?

1. Ask your female employees to list examples of someone being considerate towards them. Can

you incorporate any of their examples into your offering or training?

2. Can you incorporate the changes as a way of life and not a marketing tactic?

3. If the woman coming in the door was related to you, how would your approach change? Match that for all female customers.

4. Does the website provide more visuals than specifications? Is it easy for women to weigh options?

5. Do you sincerely apologize for being late, not being fast enough, or not responding quickly enough?

6. How do you thank your female customers? Do they walk away feeling sincerely thanked or like just another number? (mass produced posters, don't convey it)

7. Is your staff schooled in the art of helping a sale vs. closing a sale?

8. Do you respond in emails with a conversational tone, or as a business professional?

9. Do you encourage her to think out loud and consider options without getting frustrated?

10. How do you female employees "stay in touch"? Can you sincerely apply any of those methods with your customers without having it look like a tactic or being annoying?

8 Fun and Inspiring to be Around

Women love sharing a good joke, that's why they email each other so much, it only takes a second to pass on a smile and let others know that they're thinking of them. It also keeps women part of a group even if the group is virtual. It's easier to trust those you have something in common with like laughing at the same jokes.

"Fun" was a hard topic for our panel, however. Some of the women felt so over-stretched in their day that when asked what fun meant to them, they couldn't come up with anything. They had so many obligations to work and family that personal fun didn't seem like an option. Instead, they got their "fun" through things that happened during work or through activities with children.

For many, taking time to "make fun" seemed too much of a task, plus some felt they had to make sure the rest of their family or friends were having fun before they could really enjoy themselves. Fun times did happen; it's

> A glass of vino with friends and I am dancing, but I must face the truth that I am not a fun person anymore and the concept of fun play is a struggle.
> *Full time employee and mom, age 48*

just that they were in smaller time allotments or not what most people classify as fun, using a dictionary definition of the word.

What did fun mean to our panelists?

- Learning
- Being creative
- Watching others have fun
- Getting physical
- Escaping from reality
- Pain-free shopping

Hands-on, Feet First Learning

Who would have thought that "learning" would be considered fun? It sounds more like work, yet the women we surveyed noted it often and in many forms -- learning a new skill, learning a new language, or learning about a new country before going there. Learning was a way to expand their world. The way they were learning was what made it fun - it was hands-on, explore-at-will learning.

One woman learned how to fix up her home. She joined a local woodworker's club, started a library of books on the subject and began setting up her projects. Unfortunately, almost everything she found was male-oriented - the books, the clubs, and the stores. She never felt slighted for *not* being of the male gender, but something was missing.

8 Fun and Inspiring to be Around

She felt alone in her pursuit, which diminished the fun she could be having.

The women co-founders of Tomboy Tools® (www.tomboytools.com) understand this silent frustration and have opened up a new market for just these craftswomen - women who saw their homes as an artwork in progress. The Tomboy Tools mission is to *"teach and educate women how to become confident and competent homeowners, do-it-yourselfers and good stewards of their biggest financial asset, their home."*

Many companies are trying to accomplish this form of selling - offering products and services through education, but they are falling woefully short. Tomboy Tools created a new business model that was part Tupperware, part Home Depot, and part "show & tell." They have "trainers" around the country who hold workshops to teach women how to plaster, weld, paint, *etc*. Participants can attend to learn, then later buy the exact tools they need for the job. The tools are also selected to work better with women's smaller frames and hands, but are just as powerful.

Tomboy Tools doesn't believe in dumbing down its tools or its workshops. It just makes both more female-friendly. And, if participants are ever stuck for an answer mid-project, they can go to the online forum and ask for advice.

> Learning is fun, challenges are fun and failure is not.
> Corporate librarian age 64

What Tomboy Tools doesn't do (nor do good friends) is complete the project for them; they instruct, inspire and help build confidence, but never build the actual project. Good friends are those who give and take, not just give. Tomboy Tools' strength is their "exchange rate" of information, one that uses give and take methods with its customers vs. a top down delivery of "how to do it their way."

Creative Moments

Jobs change, homes change, spouses change, kids move on – having a favorite creative outlet is one of the few things that can be enjoyed regardless of the changes in life. Creative moments help define who women are and what keeps them grounded. Pursuing a creative endeavor stirs the soul and at the end of the day provides a sense of accomplishment.

The list of what our panel thought of as "creative" was endless - gardening, decorating their homes, collecting, painting, sewing, cooking... to name a few. All had one thing in common, the women "had control" over what they wanted to put their heart and soul into; they could give it their all or just dabble. Stack this against other things in their life, which gave them no say in the process or the outcome.

One panel member contributed, "When I'm in a creative mode, it's more of a solitary activity, but the feeling I get when things are flowing smoothly and I'm happy with the results - is like no other - it's definitely fun."

Long ago, my mother turned her love for flowers into public art. Each week she would take new arrangements to a restaurant where she worked for all to enjoy. She never took a penny for it. When I asked her why, she said, "It wouldn't

> Crafts make us feel rooted, give us a sense of belonging and connect us with our history. Our ancestors used to create these crafts out of necessity, and now we do them for fun, to make money and to express ourselves.
> Phyllis George, of stage and TV

8 Fun and Inspiring to be Around

be fun anymore; money would turn it into work." Instead, the restaurant "paid" her with gift certificates for meals. Thus she was able to have fun arranging flowers for diners and later arranging dinner for friends.

Vicarious Fun

One thing missing from the list is a reference to playing team sports. Our panelists mentioned it, but only in passing. They enjoyed sports more as an observer than as a participant. As the household caretaker, making sure everyone else was having a good time, came first. "Seeing other family members interact, whether eating together or playing their own games – that's fun," commented one panelist. "Witnessing my 10-year-old daughter in pure fun – playing, laughing, dancing and dreaming, gives me great joy," said another.

> Hosting a gathering and seeing everyone having a good time and knowing that I created that moment, is fun.
> Writer, age 43

Today's focus on scrapbooking is a huge new business because it captures those event moments when family members and friends are having fun. It allows women at the scrapbooking party to share an event she created with others. Those smiling in the pictures and the feedback she gets from the other women become part of her ongoing payment. And it makes her want to hold more events.

Working out with Mother Nature

While team sports weren't at the top of their list, our panelists did mention social sports, such as biking, hiking, swimming, running, walking, kayaking. If they had more time (and money), they'd opt for sailing, skiing, weekend camping. All of these were a means of doing something, usually with a friend or family member.

Many of our women enjoyed the tactile quality of sun, cold, wind, and even their own sweat. "I like to smell the salt water, the cypress and anise plants next to road and feel the continual wind against my face and feeling afterwards - that nice kind of tired," one woman commented. Being outside fed their spirit far more than a spinning class at the gym and it didn't take new clothes to participate.

Walking with a friend may be the number one way women like to stay in shape. First, they can do it by walking out of their house (no time lost). Second, they can do it with a neighbor and bond over tired blood, muscles and everything else going on in their lives. Working out is secondary to keeping their social connections "fit."

Escaping from Reality

Sometimes, it's the littlest things that bring a smile to our faces. For someone with no kids and a desk job, watching a two-year-old for 15 minutes is a nice break from their everyday reality. For the woman who has to watch that child all day, having 15 worry-free minutes *without* a two-year old is a big deal. Both are fun, only because they break the routine.

Years ago in an ad agency I operated, we had an office tradition called "Happy Minute." It was a small office of three people with no rules and no one looking over our shoulders. At 4:00 pm, we'd open a bottle of beer, pour it

8 Fun and Inspiring to be Around

between three glasses, divide up one small bag of potato chips, and deal out one card per lady. When happy minute commenced, we ate the chips, drank the beer, then flipped the card to see who got the high card. It may have only taken "a minute," but decades later we're still talking about it.

> Fun things make me stop and step away from the real world for a minute and breathe in whatever it is that is making a sense of pleasure wash over me.
> Stay-at-home mom, age 39

Another woman contributed this story: that her office holds its annual winter holiday party in July. By holding it off-season, it took the pressure off one-more-thing-to-do in December, so everyone could actually enjoy their holiday.

For some in our panel, just having "desired time alone" was enough, while others longed for last minute vacations where taking your toothbrush and your credit card was the extent of the planning. "Longed for" is the operative phrase. Women can't just jump in the car and go on a family vacation. There are dogs to kennel, food to get out of the fridge, papers to cancel, neighbors to inform, coaches to contact, kids to pack. Whether they have jobs or are a full-time domestic goddesses or both, the responsibilities for background preparations always seem to fall on women. That's the planning women wish they could avoid, but can't.

The "desired time alone" theme was repeated at a recent gathering held at ethel's chocolate lounge® in Chicago. The event was an after-work PJ Party which was just kooky enough to bring out the free spirits. The place was packed. A couple of the women who were regulars said that they come to ethel's because it's "quiet and comforting," a place to truly relax, where they can forget about their intense jobs for a while – noting that Starbucks with all its business people and laptops was "like still being at the office."

Pain-free shopping

Some identified "fun" as "not being work." For example, shopping was "fun" back when women had time to do it, but now it's work to look for clothes.

Let's look at what it's like to shop for a business suit at Mall of America, the biggest mall in the nation, located in Minneapolis, MN. First, you have to drive through jammed-up traffic to get to the mall and find a parking place. Then you start walking, walking, walking to get to the stores of your choice. The big anchor department stores (where you have the best chance of finding something for the working woman) are on opposite corners and those stores are laid out by "designer" labels instead of putting, say, all black suits together.

> Fun often strikes me as gimmicky, a way to add cost to something that's unnecessary or distracts attention from poor quality or other aspects.
> Retired corporate lawyer, age 57

Once you're lucky enough to find a style you like, the size you want is never the one available. So you take what's too big or too small and try it on anyway in dressing rooms that would depress a beauty queen. What's "fun" about shopping again?

You can see why women are flocking to buy online. They can search by "store," "designer," or "black suit," without once looking at their watch or hiring a baby sitter. Many sites now let women dress a virtual "them" (sort of like playing with paper dolls, only you're the doll). Finally,

8 Fun and Inspiring to be Around

they can order the size that they want and easily return it in the mail without putting up with a surly, underpaid customer service clerk.

> Shopping for clothes that are all designed for 20 year olds with great legs is definitely not fun.
> — Marketing director, age 52

In an odd irony, by making the mall "fun" to walk around in, it became a pain to shop in. Retail stores are reporting 20% less traffic than a year ago. Thus, by focusing on the product and not the "store experience," shopping and buying clothes online has become fun because it's less work.

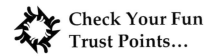 **Check Your Fun Trust Points…**

Where do you have common ground?

Where can you be reciprocal?

What's the laugh factor at your company?

1. Do women think that your company would be a blast to work for? Why? If not you, then which company in your industry do they think is great?

2. Are women inspired or drained after contact with your company?

3. Can you match her enthusiasm for a project? Do you give her a place to show it off (offline and online)?

4. How's your conversational exchange rate with your female customers? Are they fully engaged? For every action they give you, do you give back an equal action, either in person or on the web?

5. Do you host gatherings like forums, blogs, and offline places where they can compare notes with others?

6. What's the most creative use of your offering? Can you show it to other women?

7. Do you give your staff awards for coming up with their own self-propagating fun? What's their best "happy minute?"

8. What would your female customers or clients say is the "anti-fun" part of your business? How can you change that?

9. When someone visits your store/office/website – what makes them smile, every time?

10. How painless is your online and offline shopping? If not super-easy, can it be made into a mini-escape for the creative types culminating in an on-site party or contest awarding the winner a tandem bike trip with Lance Armstrong to NY or a chance to host Saturday Night Live? Too much? Okay, but you get the picture; loosen up, and your female customers will as well.

9 Safe to be "Me" with You

Feeling safe has nothing to do with being strong or weak; it has everything to do with what happens in the society surrounding women.

According to pollsters for the both the Bush and Kerry camps during the 2004 presidential election, 58% of the women and 38% of the men thought the government didn't give enough attention to the prevention of violence. The point gap is indicative of how threatened women feel.

The Department of Justice reports that 95% of the victims of domestic violence are women. While such trauma may not be part of every woman's life, stories of abuse become part of their culture, making them more sensitive to the issue.

Norah Vincent, a reporter for the *LA Times* put herself to the test for her recently released book, *Self Made Man* (Viking Adult, 2006). She cut her hair short, added a stubble beard, took voice lessons and went "underground" to experience life in the male culture. One thing that surprised her was the lack of attention she received walking down the street. Men sitting on doorsteps, who normally stared at her regardless of what she was wearing, now looked away. As a "he," she became invisible to them. A man in the same position, with women staring at him, might think, "Maybe I'll get lucky tonight..." vs. a woman's worry that, "Maybe I'll get mugged."

This is worth noting for men in sales who wonder, "What did I do?" when women distance themselves from them. Often the answer is, "Nothing." The women are being cautious, just as they would be in a ramp garage with broken lights. This means men need to work harder at showing their non-threatening side during a first impression.

Protecting Each Other

Fear for their physical safety is common ground, for women. Women don't see each other as "weak" for being wary of dark streets, hotel rooms, or parking lots. That's an accepted reality, and one where they will watch out for one another.

> You are a safe friend to me. You are protective of me and I am protective of you, kind of that mother lion mindset.
> 911 Operator, age 55, to another panelist

It reminds me of the television documentary I caught. A test was set up to see who would step in and break up an argument between a couple composed of a man and a woman. They wanted to see what outsiders would do if a man was verbally attacking a women in a public area like a park. Over and over, women physically stepped into the situation and engaged the couple.

On the male side, one man stood nearby and pretended to be talking to someone on his cell phone, but offered no direct engagement. Other men steered completely clear.

Later, the producers interviewed those people who came into the videotaped range. The women gave different reasons for engaging the couple and the men gave different reasons for not engaging them, yet the result was the same: the women DID and the men DIDN'T. The common experience of feeling unsafe themselves gave the women more empathy for the situation. They didn't want to see it escalate. "She would have done it for me," said one.

The men felt it was better to leave the couple to their own "private" argument. Perhaps if the argument had become physical, the men would have reacted differently. We won't know because it didn't get to that level.

What's the trust point?

Women will react more quickly to protect others. If companies want to be viewed as trusting, they need to react faster to potentially harmful situations.

One panelist told how she had ordered the wrong printer ink from her online source. She discovered this mistake because a woman at the company called her to ask if that was really what she wanted. "You never ordered that before so before I ship it, I thought I'd give you a call and ask," said the woman in charge of shipping. The panelist wondered – if it had been a man in charge of shipping, would he have bothered to make the call?

Fight, Flight or Group with Your Gal Pals

At one time, scientists thought that fight or flight were the only logical reactions to an unsafe situation. Then studies with women found a third option – group. It seemed that women under stress grouped up with friends when they were in an unsafe situation. Why would this happen with women and not men?

It turns out that being with others decreases stress for women, as much as running away or fighting it out does for men. One of the biological explanations for the grouping factor is the hormone oxytocin. It's a feel-good hormone that is released during maternal moments such as breast feeding or holding a baby. It's also released while making love, hugging a child or talking with a friend. (For the record, men release it also, but at a lower level.)

One company has gone as far as to market oxytocin as "Liquid Trust," saying that putting a drop of it on your hand in the morning will make people trust you all day. *"Without realizing why, the people around them have a strong feeling of trust. They can't explain it, but they know that Liquid Trust is doing its magic!"* VeroLabs is behind Liquid Trust and has posted articles from "trusted" sources like *National Geographic* to back up their claim.

It sounds like snake oil, yet women do trust and feel safer with other women, so maybe there is something to it. Psychologists report that a combination of drugs and "talk therapy" is what brings people out of depression. If oxytocin is indeed "the trust chemical," and it's released during social grooming occasions, then perhaps it's another reason why word-of-mouth marketing is so effective. Friends are already feeling good about the person they are with. When that person recommends a product, friends feel good about that as well.

I'm Okay, Just the Way I Am

Why else do women find other women safe? We return to our panel for answers. At first glance, our panel was all over the place defining what "safe" meant to them, but like all things that appear chaotic at first, a pattern eventually emerges.

Our pattern of responses fell into two piles:

1. **Acceptance**
2. **Candor**

Women accept their friends with foibles attached and feel safe because of that mutual exchange.

Regardless of how messy women's lives or homes are, feeling safe with a friend meant, "I'm okay, you're okay." Acceptance meant embracing the whole woman as she *was*, *is* and *will be*–and knowing that whatever happens in the future, that won't change the acceptance level.

> My friend accepts me and what is important to me, and even if it *IS* a bad day or a bad idea, or an inconvenience – my thoughts and deeds and dreams and fears are *SAFE* and cherished by her as PART of me.
>
> Teacher, age 52

Acceptance also meant not having to edit words or worry about how crazy their ideas might sound. Just as their appearance didn't matter, how their ideas made them "appear" didn't matter, either. They were just part of flow that made them "them."

Here's the irony and the challenge for business: If women feel safe with those who accept them just as they are, how do companies make money selling women something that tells them that they aren't okay?

Dove® did it with their "real beauty" campaign using everyday women with less than perfect bodies, and age-relevant wrinkles rather than air-brushed models. While other beauty campaigns focus on Venus-like perfection, Dove's message is, "You're fine as you are. Let's start there." It's the difference between saying, "I like you BUT..." and saying, "I like you AND..." The first dismisses and negates; the second acknowledges and builds. The first says, "You're not good enough." The second says, "You're fine and getting better."

That's acceptance.

Accepting Women's Communication Style

I attended a virtual meeting for "NEW Entrepreneur" where "NEW" stands for *Network for Empowering Women—"helping women ignite business and fuel their soul."*

The first thing NEW does at a physical or virtual meeting is allow time for members to acknowledge other members' accomplishments. As member after member acknowledged one another, I couldn't help but think how that tradition would never fly in a corporate setting. My second thought was, but this *is* exactly what women would do if they didn't have to follow the corporate model. Women willingly appreciate and acknowledge one another.

The acknowledgments lasted a good long time, but listening to everyone talk and tell her story did make you feel safe and among friends.

Candor with Can Do Support

Our panelists expected candor from their friends and, at the same time, support. Women felt safe with friends who not only gave them a solid appraisal but did so without stripping their spirit.

Being candid was essential. When women shared a project, they wanted comments back, and more than a cursory nod.

> To feel safe is not having to carefully choose my words all the time.
> Artist, age 54

It demonstrated to them that what they were doing was being taken seriously, and that their friends cared enough about them to give them helpful feedback – good or bad. The women were treated as fully-functioning adults who could make decisions based on real knowledge, not on watered-down opinions.

While the women wanted to know the truth, they wanted it delivered in a kindly manner. They felt safe knowing that

> When I knew the appraisal was from the heart, I felt safe.
> Media sales rep, age 48

friends cared enough to cushion the comments so instead of being depleted, their spirit would be renewed and revitalized. Any questions would be focused on the ideas, not the person offering the ideas.

How does being candid work with female customers? The founders of www.Awesome-Women.com sum it up best:

> "Although we saw ourselves as 'outspoken' women already, we realized how often we didn't talk about our true feelings, perceptions and internal tugs-of-war. We discovered our 'good girl' habits were deeply ingrained. We saw how much we stifled our voices because we didn't want to *'raise an issue,'* or because *we assumed no one would listen*."

The reality was that even among friends, the ability to speak freely was difficult–not because the friendship wasn't there, but because the training *not* to speak their minds was. They felt safe to be open with comments, although it took awhile before they would truly express their opinions.

Think about that the next time you run a focus group for an hour. Are you really getting the answers that you need to know? Think about it when you ask a female customer what she needs. Realize that there is a difference between being "outspoken" and being "candid." Being braver and louder than the rest doesn't mean it's the most honest opinion they have.

Safe to Lean On

Is your service center something that women can turn to in bad times, like a good friend? First of all, is it even available? Breakdowns, product failures, and mistakes never happen at convenient times. Women, especially busy moms, have no time and little patience for unresponsive customer service representatives. First, these women probably haven't had a solid night's sleep in months, and second, they're generally trying to holding a squirming toddler while attempting to take notes, all the while holding a phone to their ear.

If "customer service" is open, is there someone to talk to—*really talk to*—who is knowledgeable and empathetic? How often have you been referred to a customer service menu where none of the options fit the problem you have? If you're in the middle of a crisis, like a broken water heater leaking across the floor, do you want to connect with a long list of menu selections or a person?

> Safe with a product means it does what it says it will do and there is a person to back it up.
> Teacher, age 51

If it were up to our panel of women, they would abolish those long lists of menu selections, then take some advertising cash and move it over to customer service. As jobs go overseas and cash tightens up, more families will be making do with the products they already own vs. adding new products. In that case, great customer service will win them over. Our women felt safer with the products that had live customer service support, knowing they had someone to call who actually cared and wanted to help resolve the problem.

In fact, our panel felt that having a long list of menu options sent the message that the company is trying to hide something. By making it so difficult to reach a customer service rep during "service" times, the conclusion was that the company wasn't providing safe products to begin with.

One woman revealed how she ordered a new cell phone only to find out that it wouldn't work inside her home. No one at the cell phone company wanted to help her resolve the problem. The company didn't have a phone number to call on their main website, only email (which they weren't responding to). The local company, where she bought it, wasn't able to help her technically and didn't offer any other solutions.

Her cell phone is her personal and business lifeline and safety net. Not taking "I can't help you" for an answer, she eventually went into the company through a back corporate door and managed to reach a young woman who did help. For 30 minutes, this young women, who wasn't in customer service, searched for a tech person. She didn't put the customer on hold, instead, she set her receiver on the table so our panelist wouldn't be disconnected. Then, she used her personal cell phone to dial around internally until she located an in-house tech person.

The customer thanked her profusely for her time and diligence. Her cell phone angel said back to her, "Women have to watch out for each other because no one else will."

Postal Service?

If lack of service sets off the "trust-o-meter" for a product, think of what it does for a business whose only offering is *service*.

As we saw in Chapter One, feeling safe with a company is paramount to giving the company our business, from

9 ❀ Safe to be "Me" with You

a woman's perspective. Women feel safe with those who hold a track record of looking out for them. Looking out for them means being responsive on phone calls, following up on questions quickly, and, in general, staying in touch.

Does this sound like being "considerate"? It is. Being considerate–*with consistency*–is what makes women feel safe.

Let's look at how safe women feel about using the U.S. Postal Service, after some of the debacles during the 2005 holiday season. I know several women who have vowed never to use them again for anything except letters.

The USPS:

- Charges a premium for early arrival, but then doesn't really guarantee it. (They try; that's all.)
- Can't trace packages quickly if they don't show up.
- Makes you wait 30 days before you can put in a request for payment on insured packages.
- Makes you wait again to be reimbursed.

Meanwhile, the person waiting for the gift is stuck waiting several months. And ... the time spent running madly to get things shipped out on time, is now time lost.

Can you lean on the U.S. Postal Service for consistent service? Not this year. Would you trust them with your most important packages for business or perhaps a grandchild's birthday gift? Our panelists wouldn't.

If there were a list of reasons why going online to shop and ship holiday gifts was easy, "guaranteed delivery" would have to be at the top.

Safe Keeping

What about money? A study of more than 1,000 midlife women in 2005 by Prudential Financial found that 95% of them were either solely or jointly responsible for IRAs compared to 61% in 2000.

Women's business divisions are being formed by Merrill Lynch, Charles Schwab, Citigroup and others. The brochures are gorgeous, the advisors are trained in "Woman Speak," the class materials are well presented and yet women still ask their friends for a recommendation.

Midlifers don't have time to make up for poor business moves as they near retirement. They require someone who will watch their backs and give them advice, without making them feel stupid. News reports about women being scammed out of their life savings make them extra cautious, as no one wants to live their last days on the streets. It's no wonder they turn to each other for ideas on who they can trust.

"Fear not, Help is on the way"? Maybe.

There is so much new information on the Internet and in our email that no one knows what to believe anymore. That in itself is fearful. The one source that has all the answers also leaves many with more questions. The warnings I get in my email make me wonder if plastic wrap is safe? Will it drip some horrible toxin onto the hotdogs I just put in the microwave? Are the hotdogs okay to eat? Will the microwaves "get loose" and give me a heart attack? Will the paramedics come save me if my insurance doesn't cover them? If I get to a hospital, will they reject me at the door? It's enough to put any well-informed consumer over the edge.

Fear sells. That's why marketers use it. Maybe it's time to focus on the positive, however, and create an atmosphere that feels safe. That's what women trust.

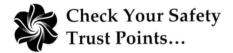

Check Your Safety Trust Points…

Where do you have common ground?

Where can you be reciprocal?

How secure do you make her feel?

1. How will she know if something is physically safe to use? Whose word does she take? Yours? The opinion sites? The government site? Blogs? Do all sites say the same thing? What are the women on those sites saying?

2. How do women know if your advice is sound after having access to the above? Can you give her five or more references using your offerings?

3. If you hold an educational meeting, will 10 or more women be in attendance? (First for the fun factor, and second for the safety-in-numbers factor.)

4. Does she feel that you would defend her if needed?

5. If 10 women saw the front page of your website and the front page of three competitors for five seconds, which one would appear most trustworthy? Put it to the test and see. Whoever they call first, is the one they trust the most.

6. Do you support her through the decision making process? Do you give encouragement along with information?

7. What would turn up if you Googled, "Unsafe (your product or service)?" Have you ever done a keyword search on Overture.com to see what terms people are linking with your name?

8. Regardless of her lifestyle, do you accept that style "as is?"

9. Are you candid but kind with her—whether you're discussing financial statements or flowers?

10. What if something goes wrong? Who does she contact? When? Are they local or long distance?

10 Honest with Her from the Beginning

One of the hallmarks for women feeling safe is to be accepted as is. It is no surprise, then, that one of the first things women wanted from friends was for them to also "come as they are," free of agendas and attitudes. It was the best way to establish common ground, without hidden agendas or potholes.

Some may think that's a leap in spirit, but I don't think so.

Those who are willing to be accepted as they are, radiate confidence. They know what they have to offer the world is unique and can stand on its own. Their personality is set and they have long since stopped trying to be all things to all people. The best chance of having a friend you can share reciprocal experiences with, is to find one you can trust on face value. The difficulty is finding that authentic face.

Let's be honest

A salesman once told me, "You know, I've been told that I'm the genuine article." To which I replied, "Really... and did they tell you what that 'article' was?"

In the same light, for some people, being honest is synonymous with being "ethical" – which is true, if you're ethical to start with. Saying you're honest isn't enough, any more than saying you have a quality product. Women have heard every line and every promise before. They need more than, "Honest, you can trust me ..."

For our panel, being "honest" meant full disclosure, no secret lives. They didn't care if the "open book personality" had torn pages, or if they didn't agree what was written on each page. They only cared that they could believe what was written.

In Dale Carnegie's book, *How to Win Friends and Influence People*, his premise was to be yourself first and always speak from experience. He was saying that speakers should speak from their "truth," a place they were less likely to be nervous in, and, a place where no one could question their authority.

The truth helps speakers in other ways as well. By shrugging off any signs of nervousness, speakers also shrug off the "tell" that they are lying. Anyone who plays poker knows what "tell" is. It's the tiniest of signs that indicates when someone is bluffing, like rubbing an eye, or stroking a chin – some common, almost invisible action, yet perceivable to a receptive observer.

"Know yourself, be yourself" is sage advice when it comes to being perceived as "honest" with women.

We've already identified that the female senses pick up more information. When you marry that to increased life experiences due to education and careers, those gut feelings become even more fine tuned. Often women don't understand why they don't trust someone, they just don't.

You can't fake who you are and if you don't completely believe that a product or service will work, placing a "sales" personality or pitch over the top of it won't help. Not in the long run and not in this new marketing environment. It's much like working out at the gym: if you're a weight lifter you build more muscle; if you're a swimmer or runner you'll end up leaner, but your structure doesn't change.

Adding more fluff to a bad product may make it sell better during that moment, but at some point it will implode as word gets out.

Recently, I watched a women give a presentation on a financial product. The first thing she did after introductions was to disclose her background, including mention of her kids and the frustrations of raising them. It wasn't a tactic, it was her being her. She followed with an educational presentation citing examples of where her financial product was a good fit for some people and not for others.

As an afterthought, she related how her financial product category had recently come under fire in the press. A key columnist had lampooned the industrial group, saying the executives "should be hauled off in handcuffs for selling it." The CEO of the company (against the legal and PR department's advice) met with the columnist and explained how the product worked. It was a big gamble, but in the end, the product's integrity and the CEO's integrity for standing behind them, not only changed the columnist's mind – she bought the product.

The pride of knowing that her product could stand up to public scrutiny, and that her CEO had the guts to stand up with it, came through. Afterwards, *when everyone else was gone*, we discussed the importance of her CEO's stand in a transparent world. She said, "I couldn't sell something I didn't totally believe in."

That's when it struck me. I've heard that phrase many times from women, and often after everyone else has left the room. It isn't a tactic, it's a personal baseline. Women in general have a hard time selling things that they don't believe in. They can't "sell" for the sake of selling for the fun of the game. It's not fun for them if the other person is losing. On some level, women know this about each other. For the women who listened to the financial product sales person speak, she was trusted more for being her honest and authentic self than for the information on her financial product. When the time comes for those women to make a purchase, she's the person they'll go back to, even if they don't remember what she told them.

Where Do Women Go for an Honest Opinion?

Women perceive honesty in their like-minded female friends through talking and learning about what they share in common. In the above case, the woman giving the presentation was a pre-approved friend of the women hosting the group. It was a case of "your friend is as good as mine."

Having a group that is "like-minded" is a key descriptor. It not only binds a group together, but is also the basis for a higher level of trust. NOP World did a survey in 2005 showing people to whom US consumers are most likely to *pass along* product or service recommendations. Friends were first on the list with 88%, followed closely by family at 87%, then people with the same interests at 66%), colleagues at 61%, and neighbors after that at 42%.

Conversely, it's logical to conclude that when someone is on the receiving end of word-of-mouth that they would recieve more information from their friends first, then family and so on down the list. The more people have in common, the more likely they'll share information. You might think that proximity would be more important, but proximity without a personal connection equals "distance." People with the same interest polled higher than neighbors.

Moms have a built-in network of friends who they depend on for information. According to a report by Lucid Marketing, which works primarily with mothers, 80% of the time they are sharing information offline. As the following quote shows, sharing goes on online, as well, and the trust rate is higher for word-of-mouth than it is for advertising.

With such a low trust rate in advertising, why didn't female consumers revolt sooner? Because, although advertising isn't perceived as honest, it's traditionally been the *only available* information women had. As consumers, women accept the fact that they are being manipulated to buy

> Pop-ups, spam and, telemarketing have a distrust level of 94%, while WOM has only a 12% distrust rate.
> Source: NeilsonBuzzMetrics

something and that some products will contain more "snake oil" than others. With the Internet, however, women don't have to buy the first snake oil shown to them. They can check out hundreds of competitive oil brands in seconds, as well as who bottled that oil, which snakes it came from, and where those snakes live.

The next question becomes, "With so much information readily available on millions of products and services, why do women *still* ask friends for advice?"

Because A) women *trust* their friends and B) friends *save them valuable research time*. But something else happens during the asking: C) each woman is honoring that friendship by demonstrating how much she values her friend's opinion.

Women also ask for opinions more often than men, first because they're more comfortable doing it; second because they have larger circles of friends which provide a bigger base of knowledgeable people. Because they keep in touch, they don't see it as imposition or a sign of weakness to ask another for advice. In fact it's more a sign of respect for the cumulated knowledge the other women hold.

I'm a living example. Not long ago, my car's warning lights came on. Although I've lived in southern California for three years, I don't have a mechanic. I could have used the yellow pages, which were sitting inches from me, as well as the Internet, to locate one, so what did I use? Neither. I called a friend and asked her for a recommendation. My reasoning was, if she used them, the service would be good and the pricing fair. I trusted her opinion. Those very same things might have been stated in an ad, but the ad couldn't validate them like she could. In a small way, I also validated her – by asking her opinion I acknowledged that I value what she knows.

Truth *is* Better than Fiction

Female friends – real friends – admit when they've made a mistake. They recognize the responsibility that comes with the trust their friends put into them.

When Oprah chose to promote the book *A Million Little Pieces* by James Frey, then later found out that it was a work of fiction rather than a true memoir, she dedicated an entire show to the fiasco. She felt duped and apologized to her audience. She could have issued a press release, but instead she looked into the cameras and into America's homes, and apologized for not standing strong on "truth." Then she told us why the truth was so important.

This is the quote Oprah read from *The New York Times,* as written by Michiko Kakutani: "This is not about truth in labeling or the misrepresentation of one author… It is a case about how much value contemporary culture places on the very idea of truth." To which Oprah added, "And I believe that the truth matters."

On her own show she confronted Mr. Frey with his lies and asked why his publisher Nan Ralese of Random House didn't vet the book before publishing it as a memoir.

To underscore the seriousness of the concern, she also brought on journalists from *The New York Times*, *Time Magazine, The Washington Post,* and *The New York Daily News* for their impressions of truth and what should have been done. As a former reporter herself, she understood what was really at stake. Her reporter's nature told her to report the facts. She did so, and by being herself and being open, she regained the trust of her audience, putting a little more truth back into America's value system.

Honest-to-Goodness Products

Lying about your life in a book seems pretty trivial compared to what some companies have done with their products and advertising. Today, websites, blogs, news reports, magazines, and even *friends* are bombarding women with every new "warning" that comes along. As consumers, they are left to sort it all out themselves. Now, in addition to multi-tasking, they're also multi-worrying. No wonder there is a backlash for simple, honest products and services that do what the label says they are going to do. The less women have to evaluate, the better.

This fits with what our panel said as well. They felt that products were more "honest" when they had fewer bells and whistles, and fewer buttons and software. They wanted items with fewer attitudes, less flash, less bravado and more practicality. Apparently K.I.S.ing your female customer has become politically correct – Keeping It Simple, is what women want.

Simple Electronics?

CE Lifestyles Magazine, which is focused on consumer electronics with a feminine edge, repeated the "more simplicity" trend. In 2005, they asked women in their 20s, 30s, 40s, and 50s what color cell phone they liked. The answers? Silver, silver/black, silver/black, silver/black.

(I have to admit, I rarely see a colored phone come out in an adult women's world.)

Later, a 2006 article reflected the same theme when it came to picking the top ten Consumer Electronic Devices: *"Clean lines, quiet colors, uncomplicated designs... the Zen in all of us love sweet simplicity,"* noted the CE editor. In fact, the whole February 2006 issue was dedicated to the "simple" theme, noting that technology can make things easier by not wigging women out with a zillion things to compare, and by not adding frustration instead of ease, to their day.

Women can't know if they "got what they paid for" if they don't know what they got. The fewer gizmos – the less there is to misunderstand, leaving fewer chances of looking stupid. Plus, there is less chance of something going wrong. This seems counter intuitive for designers, who are always pushing for the next new thing and condensing more "function" into less space.

> "It's almost a shock to the system when you actually get someone who does what they're supposed to do in the time they're supposed to and in a courteous manner."
> — IT administrator, age 49

Honest to Goodness Service – A Case Study

In the ever-changing profession of healthcare, it's difficult to determine who you can trust. Women depend on word-of-mouth to locate professionals who make them comfortable in the examination rooms and confident with their advice. That's about as personal as it gets.

When you think of the millions of dollars that go into healthcare marketing, you wonder how anyone could make a go of it outside of "the system." One female physician broke all the rules, however, and has a waiting list of patients because of it. How did she do it? It wasn't with brochures; it was by utilizing word-of-mouth advertising and by being authentically true to herself.

Dr. Susan Debin didn't want to be part of an HMO when she first started her practice 20-some years ago. She didn't want treatment for her patients determined by a corporate policy. She wanted to make her own decisions. From the moment you walk in her office, you know it belongs to a woman. The chairs, the colors, the patient "thank yous" framed on the wall—everything speaks of someone who understands women and wants them to feel at home. It isn't part of a "marketing plan," it's just Susan being Susan.

Her office has a relaxed, warm feel that carries over to her employees as well. She admits that she doesn't really manage her staff, they do what they naturally do: watch out for the patients' and each others' best interests. One day, that meant offering fresh baked cookies to patients. That wasn't part of a marketing tactic; one of the staff was hungry for cookies, made them, and offered them around just as she would outside of the office. This kind of behavior shows that although this is a medical practice, it doesn't have the sterile "medical" feel. It's relaxed and therefore the patients are relaxed, walking from waiting room to exam room as nonchalantly as if they were—well—at home.

A marketing package would stop right there, but Dr. Debin's "package" is just beginning. Most times when you're in a medical exam area, you feel like a caged rabbit waiting to be experimented on. At Dr. Debin's practice, you feel like you're meeting a girlfriend for coffee. The hallways and exam rooms carry the same "living room" atmosphere as the waiting area. Memorabilia of families and "friends" (formally known as patients) is openly displayed throughout. Hundreds of photos cover the walls; thank you notes and newspaper write-ups are posted, providing something to read besides notices about the latest dastardly disease that could kill you.

Over the years, Dr. Debin's practice has turned into a clearinghouse for anything that makes a patient "well." This all-woman's practice is open to holistic ideas as well as AMA-approved methods. Some women found having to go to another office for mammograms and other tests, was daunting. To increase their compliance for medical treatment, Dr. Debin partnered with specialists and brought their services in-house. If patients need more extensive treatment, such as surgery, Dr. Debin tries to match them up with a surgeon whose personality works with theirs.

Dr. Debin does another thing that makes her practice more personal than others – she makes sure you are called ASAP with test results on anything serious. She knows that every hour a patient waits is stressful and that one timely call can take that stress away. She's honest about what she finds and she's careful to provide all options for treatment – including holistic approaches, a practice many women appreciate.

Her dedication as a doctor and a woman is felt throughout her practice. Her authenticity translates into someone women can trust. The M.D. may have provided the way, but her honest feminine approach provides the means to really touch the patients. She has commented that early in her practice, her male colleagues would tease her that they were going to start wearing dresses. They missed the point: dressing up the business isn't enough if the heart and soul isn't part of it.

Dr. Debin's whole practice is one that creates and maintains a feeling of trust–from the lobby to the examination rooms, to her professional partners, to her staff. Honesty–and being authentic to who she is–*is* her best policy.

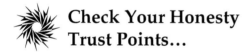 **Check Your Honesty Trust Points…**

Where do you have common ground?

Where can you be reciprocal?

Honesty is the best policy, except if being honest crushes the spirit.

1. What is the authentic, core part of your business that benefits women the most?
2. Is this offering so well-thought-out that it could sell itself?

3. Are there any operational issues about your company that could put your offering into question – especially issues that involve women?

4. Do you reward customers for giving you their honest appraisal?

5. Do your female salespeople truly believe in your service? Would they recommend it if they didn't get a commission check?

6. If you make a mistake, do you admit it immediately even going as far as to post in a blog about it?

7. Do you keep your products straightforward and simple, so that there is less to break, less to fix and less to compare with other products?

8. Are your support services easy to understand without a lot of caveats or legal forms to sign?

9. Can you give context about how the product will serve some better than others?

10. Is the entire service consistent from the lobby to the service rooms to the billing cycle? Is the consistency experienced offline the same consistency that is experienced online?

11 Reliable Beyond Question

"Don't make me ask" could be the mantra for midlife women. By the time women reach the age of 50, they've given more hours towards home, family, community and work than any other block of society. They've been relied on to perform task after task without anyone telling them what tasks need to be done.

Consequently, women have much higher standards when it comes to a service or a product being given the "reliability" stamp of approval. They expect more to be done without prodding. After all, it's what they do all day long, 365 days a year, in some capacity or another.

Home "work"

What happens at home doesn't stay there–it gets taken into her buying world.

When a task doesn't get done "by itself," and doesn't get done "when suggested," the work gets put on the woman's shoulders. The effect on one of our panelists (quoted below) was that she couldn't relax when tasks she asked her husband to do, weren't done. That old cliché, "If you want something done, do it yourself," is alive and well in her home. She told us that she believes millions of other women probably feel the same way.

> His [her husband's] lack of reliability puts a huge strain on us. I can't relax. I never trust that something has actually been done.
> Property manager, age 47

Because she loves her husband, she tolerates this lack of reliability, but what do you think happens when she's acting as a consumer? Do you think her tolerance is the same?

What a company might view as insignificant and "just business," becomes a thinly buried thorn in her side. Just because she "loves the one she's with," doesn't mean she *has* to love the product or service she's with, if it isn't reliable.

Wouldn't it be nice if a company took over tasks without her having to ask? Think how delighted she would be if a company behaved that way!

Caretaking for the Caregiver

Where else are women relied on without question? Caregiving.

Just about the time the kids are launched, aging parents and in-laws need help. In 60% of the cases, women are the ones who assume that responsibility; women provide more hours of care than their male counterparts, according to a survey by the Association for the Advancement of Retired People (AARP).

Often, those same women are so pulled between their jobs and their responsibilities to their families that they cut work hours to get in more care hours, adding financial burdens to the emotional and physical sacrifice.

If companies took time to notice that this extra effort and its importance to their female employees' lives, it would be a big acknowledgement. Women freely give one another support in this area. They take care of the caregiver and for that, they become trusted friends. Why can't companies do the same?

Volunteerism

What about volunteer activities? The fabric of civil society is held together by the millions of hours donated by women who give their skills and time to help others. Volunteer groups rely heavily on women to get this done.

At one Atlanta hospital, more than $10 million was raised by a volunteer corps made up of 99% women. Year after year they organized and raised cash to keep the children's unit funded. That hospital and hundreds of other hospitals rely on such volunteers to keep them operating and connected to the community.

Repeat that same dedication in countless other volunteer activities that rely on women to get things done. The women aren't paid to do it, but they do it anyway.

What if a company volunteered some free time to her in appreciation for what she does for all? What if a company took half of its advertising dollars (money that pays for ads women don't believe anyway) and put those dollars into something women do believe in? How much free word-of-mouth do you think that would generate?

Are You "There" for Her?

Midlife women consider a good friend someone who is always there for them. At this stage in their lives, they have a handful of friends who have stuck by them – through sickness and in health, through divorces and new jobs, through every trial and every tribulation. These gal pals may not have been part of their day-to-day life, but when needed, they were there. No questions asked.

Likewise, women don't expect companies to be part of their day-to-day life if it isn't appropriate, but when something goes wrong, that's when the "reliability" code hits. Can they call, fax, email, write to and get help? How soon and at what level the company responds will determine if you are really "there" for her or not.

> I'm not going to stick by a product or service, or believe they're sticking by me, if they don't deliver on their promise of goods and/or services.
> IT manager, age 45

One women commented, "I didn't know how loyal I was until my cell phone broke." How that reliability issue was handled determined whether she remained loyal.

Responsiveness...
Beyond the "Call of Duty."

What could possibly be different between what's reliable for women and what's reliable for men? Don't products or services merely have to work properly for both, to fall into that category? Yes, but the reliability challenge may fail at the onset if a salesperson or website can't pass the first "female-friendly" test – responsiveness.

As we've mentioned before, a common ground for women is their conversational and social style. With that comes a higher expectation to return phone calls or emails, or show up on a timely basis. And, if responsiveness can't be done in a timely fashion, apologies for the delay are expected. This is part of a woman's "Be nice" culture.

Today, there is an on-going debate about whether women in the corporate world have unlearned this civility. The reality is, some women do seem to have forgotten their roots, but their loss doesn't erase what female "consumers" appreciate and notice.

I am not saying women instantly trust someone who returns a telephone call, but I am saying that trust goes down a notch with a slow response. In her very fast moving world, "timeliness" sits next to Godliness. If someone can't do something as simple as returning a phone call in a timely manner, the customer is left wondering how reliable they'll be if given the entire job.

Positive Forces at Work

Fortunately, it isn't that hard to be proactive and put out a positive experience. One panelist gave an example (left) of how actions speak louder than words—and it was a good thing since she was having trouble understanding the language anyway.

> I chose my car mechanic because even though I can't understand a word he says (he's Asian), he gives a 10% cash discount. He has a clean room set up as an office with access to the Internet, phones, and music and he always makes sure to bring me the defective part or take me out to the car on the rack and show me why I should pay to have this 'whatever' done for my safety. I appreciate that.
> — Printing sales rep, age 48

For her, reliability came down to how he included her in the process of what was wrong, he was "there" for her by watching for things going wrong, plus he made his place "homey" enough for her to continue her work while she waited. Last of all, he rewarded her for paying in cash, which was a win/win for both of them.

Another panelist reported how she hedged her bets when her home needed repair services. Experience had taught her to call 6 to 8 professionals (handyman, electrician, plumber) to do perform work on the same day so she wouldn't waste her time on no-shows.

> You can bet that only 2-3 are even going to show up, but they all act better if they are all there at the same time—and I get more information.
> — Corporate manager, age 54

Later, when comparing two of the services performed, she said that though Job A was completed to spec, Job B was completed to spec *and* the service people were cordial during the installation. Consequently she considered Job A–"good work," but wasn't willing to give them a recommendation. Job B got kudos for, "Great work" and got a solid recommendation.

What a difference it makes to be friendly! What I'm demonstrating here is that when women give a recommendation, they're not only recommending the work but the positive feeling they received from the experience. You wouldn't expect a woman to recommend a grouch to a friend, would you? Grouches wouldn't be "reliable" for providing a positive experience and that would reflect badly on more than the product or service, it would reflect badly on her!

I Do Recall…

Let's look at companies that spend millions advertising high-end cars like Lexus. At what point do the product, the presentation, and the pitch determine reliability? The financial planner in the quote below describes her expectation of reliability in a Lexus:

In a way, this woman is saying "Don't make me ask…" She not only wanted to rely on the car, but to rely on the sales' "pitch" as well. Lesson learned? Transmissions can be replaced a lot faster than trust.

> A reliable product meets expectations. When my Lexus was "sold" to me as capable of driving 200,000 miles, it no longer met the expectation of reliability following the 2nd transmission in less than 50,000 miles. Hey, I simply forgot to ask how many transmissions were needed to reach the 200,000 mile expectation…
>
> Financial planner, age 47

If Oprah can be taken to task for unknowingly supporting a book of fiction passed off as non-fiction, certainly Lexus should get the same treatment. Especially if its sales organization promised 200,000 miles, but the car needs two transmissions before the 50,000 mile mark. Where does accountability start and end? Since this was one person, though, there will be no recall except that of an unhappy customer recalling her bad experience. They sold her one car, but they won't sell her two. (I hear she is now happily driving her second Nissan Maxima with 97,000 miles and no problems.)

The lesson learned here is that this woman didn't expect perfection in service, just someone to stand behind their product.

> When they [Behr Paint Co.] learned their Primer did not meet my expectations, they sent professional painters to my do-it-herself project and repaired the job. At the same time Home Depot, whose paint department "sold" me the paint, could have cared less about the end result.
>
> Financial planner, age 47

Let's look at two more examples of service wrapped in one project (left), where Behr Paint gained customer loyalty and Home Depot went down a notch.

Can we expect her to buy Behr Paint again? Sure. They stood behind their product and volunteered their time to help her fix her problem, exactly the way a best friend would. Home Depot? They get the less female-friendly check next to their name.

Consistent, Consistent, Consistent

For men, having a high "performance" rating, as in the Lexus, is often proof enough of what makes a product "reliable." Technical excellence was never mentioned by the women, however. Not as a top of the mind issue. For them, consistency built up not only the honesty factor,

11 ✻ Reliable Beyond Question

but also the reliability score. This meant consistency in advertising, as well.

As one of our panelists noted:

The concept of new and improved can be misleading. Think of it this way, if an old friend came to your door dressed in something completely out of character, you'd wonder what was up. Let's say she's always been an earth-mother-type and suddenly she's dressed to the nines, complete with stiletto heels.

> "New and improved" often isn't. I select a product for its particular characteristics and results so a change in the product usually prompts me to try other products to compare them – shop around. Product loyalty is lost when the product changes. Some people like change – I don't. As long as something is working well, a change only means having to expend time and energy to decide whether to adjust to the revised product or change products.
>
> Non-profit director, age 57

The person you're looking at has the same face you're used to, the same eyes, nose, smile… but the image no longer matches because the rest of her doesn't compute in your brain. The same is true of a product. Dressing it up in a fancy new package strains the credibility. It isn't what women have been led to expect – leading them to wonder, are they being duped? Midlifers aren't stuck in their ways; they just want things to work right every time without having to guess at the outcome.

This exact problem happened to me when I tried to buy new soft contact solution. The package I normally buy had been redesigned. Though it was sitting there on the shelf with 25 other kinds, I never saw it (I'm guessing it was there; I couldn't tell). Because some cleaning solutions, if not neutralized, feel like battery acid in your eyes, I'm careful about buying a reliable product that will clean the lens, but not hurt my eyes. So, I read all the labels for about 10 minutes but not one of them told me what I needed to know: could I wash and wear with this solution or did I need to wait several hours for it to neutralize?

The packaging was barely human-friendly, let alone female-friendly. The lack of straightforward information was frustrating, given my need to protect my eyes from damage. In the end, I picked one and called the company's 800# (located on the package) to get an answer. And yes, being a good little consumer, I let the customer service rep know why I needed to call, and asked her to alert their marketing department. Never let design outweigh the product's attributes. Women are practical first – except when it comes to a new pair of shoes.

Re-lie-able

Midlife women have shopped for decades. For many, the thrill of shopping has been replaced by the thrill of not having to go through the shopping process on as regular a basis as we used to. As the old saying goes, "Some things don't wash…" Sometimes, the new clothes we buy don't wash, either, which sends a disgruntled customer back to the store after she was sure that what she'd purchased was something that would last.

The clothing industry is finally producing items that are age-appropriate without being age-defining. For midlife women, finding something that covers that criteria is almost impossible. Consequently, they want to do their best to keep favorite items in good shape. When it says "hand wash" but turns into trash-wear during the process – the item's reliability gets trashed in the process. She might love the designer label, but not when is the washing instructions written on the back of the label can't be trusted.

To combat this issue, designers label many things "dry clean only." Great, now the price just doubled or tripled over the lifetime of the product. Not only is the cost not reliable, but the product is so fragile that it can't take long-term wear (That's what "dry clean only" meant to one panelist.) What's reliable about that? It's like having a fair-weather friend, and who needs more of those?

Quite a few panelists mentioned prescription drugs as examples of product unreliability. Their concern was not only for the truth behind the drugs' manufacturing, but how news reports questioning the drugs' effectiveness cast doubt on other products and services. If prescription drugs, after years of testing and approvals, are unreliable in their claims, what else about that company might be "untrue"?

It's another reason why women have a higher expectation for product reliability than men. Call it "red car syndrome" (when you buy a red car, suddenly you see all the other red cars on the highway, when you never noticed them before). Women can spot a bad product almost intuitively, because they've seen so many in their lifetimes. As the primary shoppers in the household, they are more tuned into what is good and what is bad – for themselves, their families and all the other consumers as well.

Reliable Word-of-Mouth – It's about Them

Women love to be helpful to other women (and the men in their lives). When they give recommendations, it means they are "experts" on the subject, whether it's for a great restaurant, a travel agency, or a cell phone. It feels good to be seen as the resident expert even if it is in just their own home. A recent report (left) shows the areas most likely to be referred via word-of-mouth.

Most likely referred to via WOM:
- 42% of restaurants
- 24.9% of movies/TV
- 16.2% of cell phones
- 15.7% of grocery/drugstore

Source: Lynn Russo, OMMA Feb. 2006

By providing reliable, consistent and enjoyable service and products, every time they spread word-of-mouth on your behalf, you're helping women feel good about themselves. In return, you gain free advertising of the best kind – a recommendation by a trusted friend.

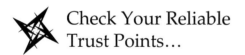 Check Your Reliable Trust Points…

Where do you have common ground?

Where can you reciprocate?

What would her girlfriends just "do" without asking?

1. Does your product or service really do what you say it's going to do? How do you prove that?

2. Do your sales people do what they say they are going to do?

3. Do you volunteer to help, as a matter of course?

4. Is your product or service one that is used 24 hours a day? If so, does your service department handle repairs 24 hours a day? (Online, this means responding to emails as fast as if someone was standing in front of you.)

5. Do you include her in the explanation of why things broke and what needs to be done next? Do you give her options and the pros and cons of each?

6. Is your personality as reliable as the service? Would it keep someone from recommending your service?

7. Are your points of distribution as reliable as you are? Will they help resolve problems on your behalf?

8. Does she have to ask for special treatment, or does it just happen?

9. Does the cost of the product include upkeep costs as well?

10. If your offering fails, how many things get added to her to-do list?

12 Thoughtful of Others in Her Global Community

Being "thoughtful" gives new meaning to "after market sales," as in: it's what you do *after* the sale that makes a marketable difference. Gal pals understand this concept completely. It's the extended kindnesses that happen throughout a friendship that set the benchmark. It may not be business as usual, but it's "life as usual," for women.

Here's how one of our panelists described "thoughtful"…

- When they hear that someone (or something – like a pet) close to you is sick or has passed away, they contact you and express their condolences and ask if there's anything they can do. And you know they mean it.
- They hear you're under the weather and they stop by just to see how you're doing.
- They try to cheer you up when you're down.

- They let you be down if you don't want to be cheered up.
- They remember your birthday/anniversary...

IT manager, age 53

It might be impossible for a company to have this close of a relationship with its customers and it often isn't expected, but women would like to think that it *could* happen.

> It seems like the older we get, thoughtful is something that becomes more important. We seem to appreciate what people do for us more than when we were young, but I also think we become more thoughtful as we age because we have a better perspective on what is really important in our lives...family, friends and a sense of community in our lives.
>
> Realtor, age 57

Even in industries where their reputation is less than stellar, such as used car sales, women still hope that *this time* will be different. That said, reputations have a way of swaying the trust factor. Sometimes, it's not you or your offering that women are reacting to; it's the reputation of the industry at large. To offset that, you need to double up on all the trust points and the contact points within her communities.

Of course, you don't have to be thoughtful if you have the corner on a market. One panelist noted how some medical specialists aren't thoughtful and make her wait; she doesn't like it but accepts it because she doesn't have a choice. But, to the medical community I say: beware! The day is coming when she will have a choice.

Bonus or Bust –

Initially, our panel had mixed reactions to the question, "What does being thoughtful mean to you?" Their first reaction conveyed general ideas about how it didn't matter one way or the other – being thoughtful was seen as a "bonus." It was like finding fresh bread and milk in your cupboard, left by a friend when you returned from a long trip – unexpected but very "thoughtful." It wouldn't make or break the friendship, but the gesture would take things to another level.

> Thoughtful service is sort of the same – that EXTRA something, (not necessarily a material thing – just customer ATTENTION) that you perhaps didn't expect.
>
> Teacher, age 55

One panelist commented how thoughtful it was of her dentist to hide the tools on a tray behind her, where she couldn't see it. "The office was beautiful and up-to-date," she said, "and the dentist was top-notch, but not seeing the tools showed me how she understood the fear factor and worked to take it down a notch."

Not in Anybody's Back Yard

Before the world was so connected, there were NIMBY (Not in My Back Yard) groups. These groups formed when someone would try to put a landfill or a cell phone tower in the neighborhood. Now that the world has grown smaller, the impact of all environmental and social issues has risen to NIABY status – Not in Anybody's Back Yard.

The panelists reflected this global concern. Being thoughtful about the greater good did indeed matter. Years ago, Grey Advertising did a survey of women to find out what was most important to them. Their first response was "a better world to live in," followed by their children "doing well."

Now that women are aware of the power of their purchasing choices, many of them are casting daily ballots with their wallet. While some of our panelists admitted that they didn't care to take the time to check out a company for its ethical or moral compass prior to buying a package of pudding, they also said they would choose a can of dolphin-free tuna over one that wasn't marked dolphin-free.

> I really prefer companies that are trying to be good to the whole world.
> Environmental safety director, age 53

They understood that the *reason* the tuna was dolphin-free wasn't necessarily because the company wanted to do the right thing, but because the company *had* to provide dolphin-free tuna or risk losing customers. Regardless of the motivation, the women were glad that the company acknowledged the problem and was trying to do better. They felt that they were rewarding the effort by buying the tuna.

No "Eddie Haskells" Allowed

Remember Eddie Haskell? If you're over 45 or watch reruns of the late 50's TV show, "Leave it to Beaver," you do. Eddie Haskell was Wally and the Beav's insincere brown-noser pal. He spent most of his time offering overdone compliments to Mrs. Cleaver, trying to curry her favor by talking at what he thought was an adult level, referring to her kids by their formal names. He wasn't fooling anyone, especially Mrs. Cleaver, who just put up with his sleazy ways.

12 ❄ Thoughtful of Others in Her Global Community

Companies trying to curry favor with midlife women through thinly-veiled attempts of "caring" will get the same eye rolls Mrs. Cleaver gave Eddie. This group has heard decades of scams and schemes and politics and promises. While they appreciate the attempt and the "causes" it might serve, if it isn't done with authenticity and sincerity, it falls into the "Eddie Haskell" file. Mrs. Cleaver didn't write Eddie off, but she silently questioned everything he said and did.

We won't name names, but you know the type of company that we're talking about. They might treat their workers unfairly, or abuse child labor laws in another country, while donating money to help develop a local park. It used to be that what happened on the other side of the world, stayed on the other side of the world. Customers weren't able to connect the dots. The Internet changed that.

Companies can avoid getting an "Eddie," by aligning their offerings with the things midlife women care about and those that fit the company's personality or mission.

Causes that Work

The Cause Marketing Forum, founded in 2002, helps companies and causes do well by recognizing good deeds. Each year the forum gives out Halo Awards to the best symbiotic matches. In 2006, some of the awards went to:

- Whirlpool Corporation® working with Habitat for Humanity® for providing appliances for the newly-built homes. Both serve the same population: homeowners.

- Music-television station VH1 gave $3.7 million worth of new instruments to school music programs. Over the last 5 years it helped 500,000 children learn how to play an instrument. Research has shown that mastering music increases a child's capacity to learn. This program not only benefited kids but it may produce the next big recording artist for VH1.

- Green Mountain Coffee Roasters®. This coffee company, which markets organic and fair-trade coffee, developed a special brand called Heifer Hope Blend and donated $300,000 to Heifer International®. Heifer International gives farm animals to impoverished families so that they can eat and profit from them. Both companies do the same thing: bring profits into third world countries and help feed the world.

- Operation Stuffed with Hugs™ gave away more than 40,000 bears to children of those serving in the military around the world, in May 2004. The bears were stuffed by visitors at the Build-A-Bear Workshops® in 170 stores and the "hugs" were distributed by the USO.

The reason these projects and partnerships work is because of their sincerity of purpose. Partnering is a win/win for all companies involved and especially for those benefiting from the hard work involved.

What doesn't Work (for us)

A Halo Award was also given to Wal-Mart for promoting more fruits and vegetables to kids. That's aligned with what their stores do, but when the company also cuts employee benefits, limiting employee access to healthcare, the "intent" looks a bit shallow. As of this writing, Wal-Mart is loosening the health insurance limits until this "PR problem" goes away. They may have won a Halo from Cause Marketing, but we're giving them an "Eddie."

Other companies we know of hosted events to raise money for cancer research yet some of the chemicals they use in their processes pollute rivers and may be contributing to employees' cancer rate. They get "Eddies" as well.

> Unfortunately, I've gotten cynical enough in my old age that I don't believe it when a product or service claims to be doing something for a cause if it helps them sell a product or burnish their public image. When [company X] pulls all their headache remedies off the shelf because someone has put cyanide in some of the bottles, that's thoughtful (well, OK, they're making sure they don't get sued too, but I think people dying was number one on their list). When [company X] makes a $1,000,000,000 donation to Save The Carp Foundation, that's publicity and not thoughtful.
> Computer systems manager, age 52

Self-Centered – the Opposite of Being Thoughtful

Many don't like hearing "glass half empty" ideas, because they focus on the negative, but sometimes that's all you have to go on. In that case, being thoughtful is accomplished by *not* being self-centered. People may not know "thoughtfulness" when they see it, but they do recognize self-centeredness and, on some base level, will steer clear of companies that exude it.

When companies continue to make unreasonably high profits; when senior level executives earn outrageous salaries and bonuses while employees lose their jobs or healthcare plans; when new plants and processes are destroying the environment—it sets a tone of self-centeredness. Women don't like helping or supporting companies that look out only for #1, especially those women who contribute so much time and energy to volunteer work to make the whole world better.

> I am just moving into a stage in my life where I loathe doing business with companies whose chief concerns are profitability and greed. I would rather go without than support any of these organizations.
> Corporate trainer, age 55

Civic Engagement

Civic engagement, or volunteering, is a new trend for men, but it's been a big part of women's lives—as much as managing a home or a corporate department. Why do they volunteer more, when they are already doing double time? Partly because their natural grouping mechanism puts them into more social interactive situations.

> "Small groups are networks," says Princeton sociologist Robert Wuthnow. "They create bonds among people. Expose people to needs, provide opportunities for volunteering, and put people in harm's way of being asked to volunteer... Even in earlier research, I was finding that if people say all the right things about being a believer [in their religion] but aren't involved in some physical, social setting that generates interaction, they are just not as likely to volunteer." Malcolm Gladwell,

"The Cellular Church," The New Yorker Magazine, September 2005.

There are other reasons for increased civic engagement, as well. First, for midlife women, they are looking for new ways to re-engage themselves when their work has become routine and/or the kids are gone. On top of that, new low levels of estrogen in their systems "unmask" testosterone, giving them a new attitude – turning the formerly meek into feisty. These women have the energy, knowledge, and time to take on new challenges. Their stories inspire one another and create a culture of "giving."

> Women are known "activists" – especially the baby boomers.
> Source: Merrill Lynch Baby Boomer Survey, February, 2005

A Friend in Need

In 1999, Lisa Amick of Orange County, CA, helped a friend take supplies down to Puerto Nuevo, a city in Mexico. The need was so great, she went back with more recyclable items the following month. Currently she goes down every month taking truckloads of usable materials such as clothes, pots and pans, and blankets.

"It's amazing how great the need is," she says. Although she has a full-time job in the hospitality business, this is her way of making a difference. People in Orange County donate things that might otherwise go into the trash. Because of Lisa's commitment, people just 4 hours south of Orange County, in another culture, benefit. Lisa says, "Everything is needed.," For example, a garage door which isn't used in Orange County becomes a roof in Mexico.

But Lisa didn't stop there.

Her co-worker, Nancy Garvey, joined her in 2000 and together they started a holiday program called, "Shoes for the Soul." While in Puerto Nuevo, they take pictures of the children, get their shoe size and put the picture and that information on top of a shoe box. Those who want to participate can buy shoes for that child and also fill the box with whatever else will fit.

Last year 450 children received new shoes and additional goodies from 450 women who already have enough. Lisa and Nancy's project isn't going to change the world, but it does change the life of those children and their families who receive the boxes of goodies. It also provides the instant gratification that comes with seeing the results of a job well done. On top of it, the 450 women who donated shoes are now aware of the bigger project.

Small Projects – Big Differences

Other projects happen much the same way that products are developed; women saw a need and did something to fix it.

An old friend of mine, Leslie Reed, is an art teacher in Kalamazoo, MI where winter comes and stays, bringing bone-chilling air and weeks of gray skies. She and her friends noticed that many of the kids coming to school didn't wear coats. It wasn't because the coats they had weren't fashionable enough to be seen in public; it was that they didn't have coats at all. That was all these women needed to see. Five of them, including Leslie, launched, "Warm Kids, Inc." and proceeded to collect and distribute over 9000 coats, hats and boots since its inception in 1986.

12 ❋ Thoughtful of Others in Her Global Community

This was done after the women performed their full-time jobs and family obligations.

These are just two examples out of thousands where women are seeing "needs" and taking action to make things better. Civic engagement or old-fashioned "volunteering" isn't a "women thing" done out of boredom; these women and others like them have full-time jobs as well as the usual home-life commitments. They are engaged and committed because they see the need and then do something about it. In turn, their efforts encourage others to join the cause or fill another need. It's a direct win for those they help, a win for them when they see the rewards of their efforts, and a win for the greater community.

> Every woman I know is more aligned to community, even those whose husbands do a great deal of "community work" (coaching, board services, etc.). Much of that in reality seems to be an extension of work and largely self-serving. Women seem to be the ones doing the less glamorous foundational work.
> — Editor, woman's business magazine, age 44

The Third Women's Movement

The first women's movement was getting the right to vote and be "heard" on a political level. The second movement, during the 60s and 70s, gave women the right to take care of themselves via access to higher education, better jobs, and the recognition that they bring more to the table than dinner.

The third movement will be on a grander social scale. Now that midlifers have taken care of themselves, they are reaching out further to their extended, world family and taking care of them, because—well... that's what women do.

Companies wanting to align themselves with midlife women need only recognize this pattern and match it *with the same dedication and sincerity of purpose.* Some might say, "That's not why we're in business," and to them I say, "See ya!"

This is a customer-based world we live in. Just as customers wouldn't put up with that selfish attitude in a one-to-one setting before mass marketing, they won't tolerate it in this new one-to-one setting made possible by the Internet and social computing.

> I gravitate toward eco-friendly, low-impact, reasonably priced products. I try to remain informed on what corporate practices are practiced by companies I support, and have been known to boycott products if their producer has negative press (based on fact).
> New Zealand "world traveler", age 54

The self-anointed "world traveler" quoted here is a woman who worked as a cruise ship librarian who set up cultural exchanges when the cruise ship would reach port. As a research librarian and cultural director, she is drawn to the "differences" that make an experience indigenous and worth the trip. It is with a certain irony that she admits that it wasn't the "differences" that made her a citizen of the world. "I know it's trite to say," she remarked, "but… we're all the same." She went on to explain that we all want love, we want to feed our families and to laugh and to share our lives – it's not that complicated.

That sameness is what connects with the midlife women here in the U.S. General Electric recently honored that concept with a commercial promoting their new sonogram equipment. It showed the mothers of the world interacting with their new babies while in the background, a woman sings a lullabye. It's called "The Power of Sound," but the real power lies in the universal appeal such an ad possess. It's real, it acknowledges the vital role that women play, and it's, well, thoughtful of their world. In this case, the "cause" is mothers, regardless of where they live.

They'll Do it Themselves

The third women's movement is already underway as midlife women are finding ways to better the world. It's no secret that companies want the female consumer's attention and as women understand the power of their choices, more women will make a conscious effort to be an "active" consumer. They'll support products, services and corporations who want to create a softer, saner world—just like they do.

They are also starting their own "cause-to-business" blended efforts, like Barbara Geraghty. Barbara is no slouch when it comes to business. As a sought-after keynote speaker and author of *Visionary Selling*, she has earned her frequent flier miles traveling to speak at Fortune 500 sales training events.

In her travels, Geraghty has seen the devastation that hit Uganda because of war and HIV. She saw it and couldn't ignore it.

In response, she launched www.wakati.org. which promotes Third World products. She could have stayed with the career and retired like everyone else does, but instead she chose to work at her consultancy, Achieve the Summit, and also help the women of Uganda fight poverty and support themselves (and what's left of their families).

Geraghty is completely dedicated. "I have stepped into the purpose, I will pursue with passion and verve for the next thirty years," she says. Barbara is a midlife woman who sees no reason to let age keep her from leaving the world better than she found it.

Multiple "Choice"

Most people know that doctors take the Hippocratic oath which boils down to, "First, do no harm." Google tries to live by the statement, "Don't be evil." If women had an oath it would be, "Look out for one another."

It's in that light that women choose who they will or will not work with. If multiple "choice" in the market is the new given (and it is when you can buy from anyone, anywhere) who will women trust? More accurately, what will they trust–a company that relieves human suffering, like they do, or one that does nothing?

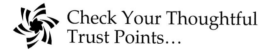 Check Your Thoughtful Trust Points…

Where do you have common ground?

Where can you be reciprocal?

What makes your company a good citizen of the world?

1. Are you using a "cause" to position yourself as a good global citizen or because it's the right thing to do?

12 ❦ Thoughtful of Others in Her Global Community

2. Would you do it anyway if no one was looking?
3. Are you in line for a Halo nomination or for an Eddie?
4. Does your company make more headlines for the good it does or for the profits it makes?
5. Do you recognize what your female (and male) employees do to give back to society? Do you enable them in those pursuits?
6. Could you put a dollar value on it?
7. Do you help those ready for retirement find a way to be civically engaged and continue the good work?
8. How do your employees look out for one another during work hours and afterwards?
9. Do you ever reward your own employees with a "just because" gift? Something that is a total surprise and not a corporate "thing"?
10. Do you take employees aside and praise them for being a positive catalyst? For being the "mom" that everyone goes to for help? For example, praising those who stabilize the office simply by being the local "guru" everyone relies on?

13 Loyalty, the Sum Total of the Trust Points

Ask someone in marketing what loyalty means to them and one of the first things they visualize is a line of returning customers responding to their "loyalty rewards program."

We won't knock incentive-based promotions; they have their place for tracking information that otherwise would be lost. But many women will agree, loyalty programs actually do very little to improve loyalty. In fact, none of our panel members mentioned them. If "love" means never having to say you're sorry, then loyalty means never having to say "incentive."

Ask women what they think about loyalty in friends, products and services and they'll say loyalty revolves around personal attention. They also want consistency (again) and an unwavering value as it plays across all the terms so far.

That is THE lesson in female customer loyalty–it isn't one term, it's all terms. "Loyalty" is the ultimate proof of what customers *really purchased* – and it was more than the product or service.

Women also see loyalty as a mutually beneficial thing. They're astounded when companies want their loyalty, yet feel no need to reciprocate.

While car companies were waving the "Buy American" flag, they were also busy buying supplies or using vendors from outside the US. Everyone knew it but everyone played along for the sake of the "team." The idea was if you buy an American car, you'll keep an American employed – which worked as long as Detroit produced products which *all* Americans wanted.

When Detroit ignored what women needed in a practical car, it opened the doors to women buying high-mileage, low-maintenance Toyotas. Yes, there were bigger issues, like trade tariffs that made the field uneven at first, but it took Detroit decades to get the message and start building something comparable. Today, Toyota is a growing automobile company with a decidedly feminine feel. The company makes cars women want, and both benefit.

Pay attention – You'll Raise Their Self-esteem and Gain Their Loyalty

Just like little "tests" make or break friendships, little tests make or break the loyalty cycle for women. When friends "kiss and make up," having worked through the problem, the friendship becomes stronger. They know the friend will stick by them the next time a similar level issue arises. The same is true for business.

13 ❖ Loyalty, the Sum Total of the Trust Points

An interesting thing happens when you let people talk out their frustrations with a company. Remember that national average figure of 7% of the population trusting advertising? When the "complainers" on Planet Feedback were surveyed as to whether they trusted advertising 16% of that crowd said they did.

Going from 7% to 16% on the Trust-O-Meter isn't that big of a leap but it does show the power of being heard and responded to. As conversation increases, trust increases and loyalty has a better chance of being maintained. Those complainers didn't have resolved issues, by the way, they were more "trustful" of advertising and, presumably, business because they were given a chance to voice their opinion. It's not any different from standing up and having your say at a town hall. Taking a stand makes people feel like they are part of the customer/vendor equation instead of feeling powerless.

By listening to someone you show tolerance. Tolerance brings out trust. Maybe the company doesn't tolerate complainers, but the public forum will. The court of public opinion can give those who speak out, vindication. Often, just feeling as if their opinions matter makes a difference in building trust. As Psychologists know, acknowledgment is one of the most powerful ways to build self-esteem. If people feel good about themselves, they are less apt to feel bad about your product or services.

When They're Happy and They Know It...

Keeping midlife women happy is, in some ways a lot easier – and in others, a lot harder – than keeping the general population happy.

As noted in the earlier chapters, midlife women have "given" to their kids, "given" to their partners, "given" to their communities, and "given" to their careers. That give–and–take issue is another common ground. Women understand that imbalance and work harder to overcome it. When a business, "gives" them back *any* attention, (such as returning a phone call) it's viewed as incredible service and remembered.

For some in our panel, just getting a bill for the price they were quoted made them surprised and happy.

Showing up on time is another issue so abused that when it happens, it's noted and gets added to the loyalty basket.

Getting information on a side issue—something that wasn't part of business on a follow-up call—was also unexpected and noted.

Little things that seem like common sense are so neglected in modern business that when given, they stick out as service that is "exceptional," "over-the-top," "incredible,"—and that's something women of any age applaud.

Loyalty to Baggage Handlers

The women on our panel didn't want to leave a company once they were happy. What made them happy and *loyal*, wasn't the product, it was "service" based on what *they* thought good service should be.

Back when people had "secretaries," it was a sign of power (and necessity) to have them handle all incoming calls. Back then, the people doing that front-end answering were usually women, and those women are now the ones standing in front of you ready to open their purses.

While being labeled *"just"* a secretary or receptionist or waitress… these women learned how to be civil and professional. They also worked five times as hard as today's front line, since everything was done by hand, on paper, or in their heads. Today, their patience is tested when, with all the technology available, the service given is lower than what they provided in those early days, *without* a computer, a blackberry or a cell phone.

Plus, as former underlings, these women have watched the power games being played and they want no part of them now. They aren't impressed with hierarchy and prefer peer-to-peer treatment. It's another reason they like working with women in their age sector who went through the same boot camp.

> To qualify as my friend… women have proven themselves exceptional individuals, ones who have been 'there' for me, and shown they 'get' what I am about. Likewise, I try to mirror those same qualities.
>
> Small business owner, age 49

Put that all together and what do you get? The unspoken measurement of how midlife women define "quality service." It's a high benchmark to reach and often companies have to withstand a lot of flack before they get there.

> I'm loyal to service because it's easy – I don't have to think. I know how it works.
>
> Appraiser, age 48

Dave Pogue, a columnist for the *New York Times*, gave a report on CBS Sunday morning in 2005 about losing his hard drive. He ended up going to the Internet and finding www.drivesavers.com. In the process, he met the lead customer service person. She was hired for her ability to deal with people and calm them down during incredibly stressful times (like losing a harddrive). During the conversation, Pogue discovered that her former job qualifications had perfectly prepared her for her new role: she had previously answered calls for a suicide hotline.

We might laugh, but losing a hard drive and everything on it could also mean losing your job, your business, your marriage… all of which have nothing to do with the problem at hand and everything to do with your personal life. In the same way, when women are calling about problems with a product or service, it's also about how the *lack* or *failure* of that product or service has disrupted their lives. At this point, they really want someone to talk to, a "real person" kind of someone.

It's something to consider if your company's product or service is tied to multiple life functions, such as the phone, car, insurance, etc. Instead of adding more telephone menu options, think about adding a HELP line and a social worker who can work with women at their level of experience.

Overcoming the friction factor

"I'm loyal to [my] bank," said one panelist. "It's tough to move all your accounts."

For her, happiness and loyalty was by default. She had a bank that was "ok," not great, but good enough for her loyalty. Offering her a new toaster or free checking wasn't going to offset the hassle of updating the will, trust, partners, children, business, financial planners, and everything else on her personal food chain, once she left the bank.

13 ❖ Loyalty, the Sum Total of the Trust Points

What would happen, however, if a competing bank offered a financial re-organizational package to go along with the switch? Not only would she get the toaster, but she would get her finances in order and would be able to implement a system to update her files, something she probably hasn't done in years.

Now she's happy *because* of a service that's mutually beneficial. She is loyal *because* someone cared enough to give her a system and teach her the basics. Instead of feeling the burden of updating, she feels the "fun" of learning and the power buzz of getting her financial life under control.

> 95% of midlife women have sole or joint management responsibilities of their IRAs.
> Source: Prudential Financial

Which customer is more loyal, the woman who stays because of the friction factor or the woman who invested in you because you invested in her?

Crossing Default Lines

When there is a crack in the service, crossing the line and telling the company what's wrong is easy for some women and difficult for others. One panelist summed it up this way when a service manager was rude to her 85 year old mother-in-law (right):

A week later the service manager called her mother-in-law to apologize. That's all it took to keep a long-time customer, an apology. The older women's culture was to

> As a teacher, I would rather have someone let me know up front if I've screwed up so I can try to remedy the situation. I told him [the service manager] whatever he decided to do was his choice, but without this information he would have no choice, he'd just have one less customer.
> Teacher, age 45

not confront the issue, just walk. The midlife woman's experience taught her to give the business a chance to make good.

When a boomer woman calls up a company to complain, she may be discussing the problem, but underneath she's thinking "I'm upset. I'm leaving, toodles. Give me one good reason to stay…" Her sense of fair play is wrapped up with getting her off the emotional hook. If she tried to play nice and the company didn't play nice back, then she's free to leave without guilt.

Don't even think about it

Many of the women commented on why they liked brand names. Ironically it wasn't the brand attributes they mentioned, it was because once they had a brand "the decision was made." The brand made shopping faster, for herself and others in her group. Brands make it easier to communicate what she wants from the family member she sends out the door: "Just get the butter in the yellow and green box." When shopping on that level, price wasn't the first consideration, convenience was.

> Like most women, I think I prefer to stay with a product if it has been good value for the money, proven to be good to its (marketed) promises, and fills a true need (not a passing fancy).
> Information researcher, age 50

Simon Delivers, a grocery delivery service in Minneapolis capitalizes on the need for convenience and attracts no-brainer loyalty. The store provides customers with a checklist of the things they buy on a regular basis. When convenience outweighs price, this is the perfect solution. Members can log in to their account and check off what they want faster than they could check out Brad Pitt inside *People Magazine*. Ok, it's not as fun, but it is one more thing off their list of mundane tasks… And they don't have to think about it again.

Long Distance Relationships

> I'm usually loyal to people based on the length of time I know them rather than the benefits we hold in common.
> Magazine editor, age 50

Our magazine editor makes a simple enough statement and although it applies directly to her friends, it also has a strong business application. With the Internet, loyalty can travel over distance as well as time. When midlife women pick up the phone or email a gal pal, no time or distance has passed. Conversely, have you ever sat next to someone on a bus or in an airport and discovered you had nothing to talk about? Now *that's* a long distance relationship.

Companies can shorten the "distance" by using the same tactics midlife women use to stay connected with each other – proactively learn about the changes in their world and how those changes affect them.

Pivot Point Turns

Creating loyalty at midlife may seem daunting at first because many companies already have a woman's "mindshare" locked in. Where other companies can get an edge is during pivot points that naturally occur at midlife. Pivot points include things like losing a partner, losing a job, gaining a job, adult kids coming home, parents needing care, personal health issues. Stuck in the middle, holding all the pieces together, is the midlife woman.

> If a woman screams in the middle of her life, will anybody hear her? Midlife women want to know.

During pivot points, all bets are off. These women may be going in one direction, perfectly happy, and then WHAM, life hits them.

WomanSage is an organization that formed just for this crowd, providing a safe place to regroup, renew, and then rejoin society when ready. It wasn't the programs that caused the women to flock to WomenSage, it was the friendships that formed. Life was going to happen anyway, but not having to go it alone made the difficult times less daunting.

In that light, having a vendor who can move virtually with them if they have to relocate, or who understands the pressure of taking hard turns at midlife, will re-earn their trust and establish a deeper loyalty.

> I am loyal to PEOPLE of the companies who have, over time, treated me with friendliness and respect. They don't always have to give me what I want, it's their attitude toward me that counts.
> Between jobs, age 51

"Facing" the Situation

Corporations, by their nature, are a cumulative effort of people all doing the best they can to put out the best product or service possible. Unfortunately, in an effort to increase efficiency, they lower effectiveness and customer contact. In a man's world, that's okay—men don't care as much for personal contact, they don't want to "ask directions" and they thrive on their independence. As the previous chapters have shown, this isn't true for women.

13   Loyalty, the Sum Total of the Trust Points

Women don't "need" faces any more than they need colorful packaging, but faces can make the difference if someone stays or goes, buys or doesn't, returns or not. Women can

> We seek each other's judgments, trusting the responses; delight in each other's successes, happiness & joys, while empathizing during turmoil, struggle and pain.
>
> Librarian, age 50

go anywhere for the news, but they tune in to the CBS Evening News and Katie Couric just to see their favorite girl-next-door reporting on the daily world events. They can buy a self-help book, or be inspired by Oprah. They can read a recipe or let Martha show them the "right" way to cook. It's Katie's, Oprah's, and Martha's face and personalities that give all three celebrities top ratings and a loyal audience.

Here's a suggestion: customer turnover due to employee turnover isn't new, but with personal interaction being such a high driver, rather than putting $2.5 million into 30 seconds on the Super Bowl, why not hire more women in customer contact points or launch a solid word-of-mouth campaign?

What we're saying here is that advertising can buy awareness but it can't buy trust. That you have to earn – and when you've done that, you also win loyalty.

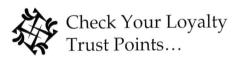

Check Your Loyalty Trust Points...

Where do you have common ground?

Where can you be reciprocal?

What makes you lose loyalty besides the cost?

1. How much personal attention do you give your female customers?
2. Are you as loyal to them as you want them to be towards you?
3. Do you encourage them to speak up, or complain, if they have a problem (offline and online)?
4. Do you let them rant until they run out of steam?
5. Do you respond to them thoughtfully and personally; can they SEE your face?
6. Are your front-line customer service people skilled not only in fielding the cause of the problem, but also in fielding her life issues, as part of their "service?"
7. Do you help them resolve the problem even if it isn't your problem?
8. Do you provide reasons for women to stay with your company, besides the high hassle factor if they leave?
9. If they moved to another state, is your business able to go the distance?
10. Do you know what the pivot points are in your female customer's life and how to help them make that turn a little easier?

In Women We Trust.
In Business We Hope.

All of these trust points make for sustainable friendships or loyal customers. It only takes one or two to get the ball rolling. Likewise, it only takes one or two to destroy that positive direction.

Not all women see the trust points the same way, their age and experience will alter their views, but the negative trust points are becoming more obvious, or we wouldn't be seeing this cultural shift. Let's review, only this time, let's look at them from the flip side.

If you are no longer inside someone's **community** (physical or virtual), the relationship dies or becomes long distance. You have to either boost the communication contacts, or be very solid in the other friendship values. Only then will a relationship be sustainable without ongoing interaction.

This leaves businesses with a choice–how do you want to be viewed: as a friend, an acquaintance, or as what's-her-name?

If you've lost **respect** for a friend, do you bother with more than polite hellos? Where does respect fit in, at your company? Are you getting polite hellos or are you greeted with happy, genuine smiles? If you aren't seeing any teeth when she smiles, that may be your first indication that something's gone south.

Are you more **considerate** of them than they are with you? How long do you remain friends with those who consider only themselves first?

Is everyone having **fun**? How long do you hang out with friends who drag you down?

Do you seek out people who scare you or who alleviate your fears? Do you offer a **safe** haven for your friends?

Do you stay friends with those aren't **honest** with you? If you do, how much harder is it for you to trust whatever they say?

We all have friends we keep who aren't **reliable**, but are they your top-tier friends or your bottom-tier friends?

Does it matter if your friends are **thoughtful**? Do you think less of them when they are completely thoughtless of you and others? There's your answer.

How **loyal** are you to your friends? Can you pinpoint a reason that tested your loyalty? Chances are it was one of the items above.

Women have learned to depend on and trust one another. In their search for products and services, they will look for companies that act in the same fashion as their gal pals. Because the women's consumer culture is shifting – to the softer side of business.

Trust is the true differentiator. Think about it – who do you trust? Who do you count on? Why? What businesses earn that same trust value? Does it matter?

At one point in the corporate world, managing your personal or business reputation was – well – everything! Somewhere along the line, reputation took a back seat and profit at any cost moved ahead.

Today's companies can't move fast enough to stay ahead of a bad reputation – and profits are following them downhill almost as fast as negative news hits the blogs.

No doubt your company is comprised of good people who, on their own, would make an honorable decision, given the choice. However, as is often the case, the decision isn't their choice to make. Instead, they grudgingly sign off on their part of the overall project to keep their job for another day. All those little decisions add up. Eventually the pile of compromises needed to get the offering out the door start eating into the value of the offering.

We're all guilty to some extent of overlooking trust points. Or perhaps, certain individuals are just ignorant of the shifting culture and continue operating as if gender didn't matter.

One of my readers for this book is the retired owner of large furniture store. As he read the subject matter, he confessed amazement. To him, this is all common sense. But admittedly, he gained his knowledge of how women think through years of trial-and-error. Hundreds of sales conversations with hundreds of women customers buying bedroom furniture showed him the way.

To be honest, I can truthfully say he made very few sales "errors." He was then and still is now, a highly effective sales person. He succeeds so marvelously because *he actually likes, respects and values people—all people*. That's not a sales gimmick or a tactic, that's something you feel the moment you meet him. It can't be gained through better advertising. His personal integrity went hand-in-hand with the store's integrity and he worked to keep both high. A poor reputation in his town would have crushed his business.

That's one example (and male at that) in a small town setting, that encapsulates the hope we have for business at large.

We think the Internet is helping business get back to that one-to-one relationship found in small town settings. Even the largest companies can keep it personal if they want to. And since individual employees can also be targets on opinion boards, they have equal incentive in becoming a customer's "best friend" and building trust. To a customer, the last person they come in contact with *is* the company. A quick read of the opinion sites shows that customers complain more about individuals than they do the company at large.

We believe that once opinion boards are as common as websites, a self-policing action will happen just as it does on E-Bay. Opinion sites may not post ratings like E-Bay, but they do create a holding ground for poor performance and who needs that on their resume?

Keeping female (and male) consumers happy and "in trust" with you is what this book is about.

In Women We Trust. In Business We Hope.

We know it won't be easy. Companies are living organisms made up of male and female minds, all making decisions based on biological and social factors. We say that if businesses put their trust in their female consumers and their female consumers feel empowered to speak up–to identify what they like and what they don't like, everyone will go home much happier and much more trusting.

The women's consumer culture is shifting. I hope this book helps you shift with it–and gain the trust, respect, and loyalty of all your customers, using our nine trust points to guide you.

APPENDIX A: COMPLAINT/PRAISE SITES

Epinions - Product reviews and business in general
www.epinions.com

Zipingo - Yellow pages with ratings; find businesses by zip code and references
www.zipingo.com

Planetfeedback - One of the original sites for general business, product and service complaints
www.planetfeedback.com

Yahoo! - http://dir.yahoo.com/ Society_and_Culture/Issues_and_ Causes/ Consumer_Advocacy_and_ Information/Consumer_Opinion/

Review Centre - Consumer reviews, price comparisons, shop ratings, forums
www.reviewcentre.com

Rip-Off Report - Enter complaints and review complaint histories
www.ripoffreport.com

CASPIAN - Consumers Against Supermarket Privacy Invasion and Numbering (name says it)
www.nocards.org

AskAnOwner - Forum for asking about products others own/use
www.askanowner.com

AskAPatient - Prescription drug and side effect reviews
www.askapatient.com

Complaints.com - Product and service complaints
www.complaints.com

Ratings.net - Ratings, reviews and reports on products and services
www.ratings.net

DooYoo? - Consumer forums
www.dooyoo.co.uk

MarketMarks - Consumer ratings service
www.marketmarks.com

My3cents - Consumer complaint/compliment site; with free letter-writing service
www.my3cents.com

The Complaint Station - Product, service, and employment discussion groups
www.thecomplaintstation.com

eComplaints - Posts compaints and company responses
www.ecomplaints.com

SafetyForum - Serves the public, media, legal community, policy makers, manufacturers, and service providers on safety issues
www.safetyforum.com

TheSqueakyWheel - Offers to create web page for complaint and send repeated emails to offending company; fee-based
www.thesqueakywheel.com

TCCL - General complaint site
www.clik2complaints.co.uk

Complaint Book - Serves as third-party for managing consumer complaints
www.complaintbook.com

uSpeakOut - Consumer experiences and opinions
www.uspeakout.com

This Is Broken - Project by Mark Hurst to show business how to fix "broken" consumer experiences
www.thisisbroken.com

Official Internet Blacklist - (again, the name says it all)
www.blacklist.com

Informercial-Reviews - Consumer reviews of infomercials and as-seen-on-TV products
www.informercial-reviews.org

Syllas Forum - Focuses on electronics, including phones, computers, home cinema
www.syllas.com

Judy's Book - User reviews of local products and services
www.judysbook.com

Comments.com - Post comments, complaints, suggestions, and questions
www.comments.com

Angry Box - Outlet for venting about issues from airline delays to presidential politics
www.angrybox.com

NetComplaints - Post omplaints or compliments on products, politics, sports, celebrities, colleges, organizations, and more
www.netcomplaints.com

Denture Wearers Action Group - Educating consumers about the difference between dentists and denturists
www.frontiernet.net/~dwag/DENTURE-PROBLEMS-GOTCHA.html

GetBetterService - Forum to bring together customers with complaints to get organizations to improve theirservice
www.getbetterservice.com

Riffs - Social recommendation and review site; vote for or against people, technology, products, movies, and just about anything
www.riffs.com

APPENDIX B: WORD-OF-MOUTH GLOSSARY

Organic Word of Mouth – Occurs naturally when people become advocates because they are happy with a product and have a natural desire to share their support and enthusiasm. Practices that enhance organic Word of Mouth activity include:

- Focusing on customer satisfaction.
- Improving product quality and usability.
- Responding to concerns and criticism.
- Opening a dialog and listening to people.
- Earning customer loyalty.

Amplified Word of Mouth – Occurs when marketers launch campaigns designed to encourage or accelerate WOM in existing or new communities. Practices that amplify word of mouth activity include:

- Creating communities.
- Developing tools that enable people to share their opinions.
- Motivating advocates and evangelists to actively promote a product.
- Giving advocates information that they can share.
- Using advertising or publicity designed to create buzz or start a conversation.
- Identifying and reaching out to influential individuals and communities.
- Researching and tracking online conversations.

Amplified WOM Terms:

- **Buzz Marketing:** Using high-profile entertainment or news to get people to talk about your brand.
- **Cause Marketing:** Supporting social causes to earn respect and support from people who feel strongly about the cause.

- **Community Marketing:** Forming or supporting niche communities that are likely to share interests about the brand (such as user groups, fan clubs, and discussion forums); providing tools, content, and information to support those communities.
- **Conversation Creation:** Interesting or fun advertising, emails, catch phrases, entertainment, or promotions designed to start word of mouth activity.
- **Grassroots Marketing:** Organizing and motivating volunteers to engage in personal or local outreach.
- **Evangelist Marketing:** Cultivating evangelists, advocates, or volunteers who are encouraged to take a leadership role in actively spreading the word on your behalf.
- **Influencer Marketing:** Identifying key communities and opinion leaders who are likely to talk about products and have the ability to influence the opinions of others.
- **Product Seeding:** Placing the right product into the right hands at the right time, providing information or samples to influential individuals.
- **Referral Programs:** Creating tools that enable satisfied customers to refer their friends.
- **Unpaid Media:** A close sister to PR, this could be a human interest story about your product or service that the press picks up, i.e. customer testimonials, quotes and success stories that agreed written about a person.
- **Viral Marketing:** Creating entertaining or informative messages that are designed to be passed along in an exponential fashion, often electronically or by email.

SOURCE: Word of Mouth Marketing Association
www.womma.com

Appendix C: Sampling of Online Women's Groups

Awesome Women	www.Awesome-Women.com
Blue Suit Mom	www.BlueSuitMom.com
Gathering of Women	www.GatherTheWomen.org
Give and Take Network	www.GiveNTakeNetwork.org
Hispanic Women Directory	www.HBWA.org
Women Rise	www.WomenRise.org
Int'l Virtual Women's Chamber of Commerce	www.IVWCC.com
National Assoc. of Female Executives	www.Nafe.com
National Assoc. of Women Artists	www.NawaNet.org
NEW Entrepreneurs	www.NewEntrepreneurs.org
Team Women	www.TeamWomen.com
Web Mothers	www.WebMomz.com
Women Can Do Anything	www.WCDA.ca
Women CEO Network	www.Women-CEO.com
Women for Hire	www.WomenForHire.com
Women in Enterprise	www.WomeInEnterprise.com
Women in Technology Int.	www.WITI.com
Women Mobility	www.WomenMobility.org
WomenSage	www.WomenSage.com
Women's Edge Coalition	www.WomensEdge.org
Women's Global Business Alliance	www.WGBA-Business.com
Women's Int'l Center	www.WIC.org
Women's Leadership	www.WomensLeadershipExchange.com
WORLDWIT	www.WorldWIT.org

In Women We Trust

INDEX

A

Achieve the Summit 145
America's Competitive Secret: Women Managers ii, 42
AARP 21, 121
American Business Women's Association 10
American Society of Women Accountants 10
Amick, Lisa 141
Association for Women in Technology 10
Awesome-Women ii
Awesome-Women.com 98
A Million Little Pieces 111

B

Balter, Dave 27
Bank Marketing International 21
Barletta, Martha ii
Barnes and Noble 13
Behr Paint 126
Berry, Jon 26
brain, gender differences 34-6
BuzzAgent 27
BuzzMetrics 24, 109

C

California Women's Leadership Association 10
caregiving 120
Carnegie, Dale 106
Cause Marketing Forum 137
CBS Evening News 159
CE Lifestyles Magazine 112
Commercial Real Estate Women 10
Community 41
Complaint/Praise Sites, App. A 167
comSource Networks 35
Considerate 39, 69
Consumer Electronics Association 21
Conway, Kellyanne 61
Couric, Katie 159

D

Debin, Dr. Susan 114
Dickless Marketing ii
Directory of Orange County Networking Organizations 8
DiVita, Yvonne ii
divorce 13
domestic violence 91
Don't Think Pink 4
Double Click 28
Dove® "real beauty" campaign 96

E

E-Bay 164
E-Marketer 26
Eddie Haskell 136
Edelman 31
ethel's chocolate lounge 87
Evolution, Alienation and Gossip 24
ewomanetwork.com 9
ewowfacts.com 21
Executive Women International 10

F

female-friendly culture 14
female brain 35
female market statistics 18
female workforce statistics 19
Financial Women International 10
Forum for Women
   Entrepreneurs 10
Foster, Jodi 60
Fox, Kate 24
Free Press 21
Frey, James 111
Fun 39, 81

G

'good girl' habits 98
Garvey, Nancy 142
General Electric 144
George, Phyllis 84
Geraghty, Barbara 145
Gladwell, Malcolm 140
Green Mountain Coffee
   Roasters 138
Grey Advertising 135

H

Haas, Jane Glenn 55
Habitat for Humanity 137
Hall, Judith 36
Halo Awards 137
Hippocratic oath 146
Home Depot 83, 126
Honest 39, 105
*How to Win Friends and
   Influence People* 106

I

Interpret-her 14, 39

J

Johnson, Lisa ii

K

Kakutani, Michiko 111
Keller, Ed 26
KN™ Pajamas 27
Kotler, Philip 29

L

Lake, Celinda 61
Learned, Andrea 4
Leave it to Beaver 136
Lexus 125, 126
Liquid Trust 94
Loyal 39
Lucid Marketing 109

M

male brain 35
Mall of America 88
Marketing to Women 4
marriage and birth rate decline,
   Australian study 55
Medical Economics 45
Men's Health 21

Merrill Lynch Baby Boomer
   Survey 141
midlife women 2, 22, 57, 102, 122
Miller, Michelle ii

N

National Association of
   Professional Mortgage
   Women 10
National Association of Women
   Business Owners 10, 44
National Association of Women
   in Construction 10
Neuberger, Karen 27
NEW Entrepreneur 96
Network for Empowering
   Women 96
New Girls' Club 40, 44
NIABY – Not in Anybody's
   Back Yard 135
NOP World survey 2005 109

O

Operation Stuffed with Hugs 138
Oprah 27, 111, 125, 159

P

Pease, Barbara and Allan 36
presidential election, 2004 91
Prudential Financial 102
putting others first 75

Q

Quick Med X 64

R

Ralese, Nan 111
Random House 111
Red Hat Society 8
Reed, Leslie 142
Reichheld, Fred 34
Reliable 39, 119
Resource Interactive 35
Respectful 39, 53
responsiveness 123
Rice, Berkeley 45
Rosener, Judy ii, 42

S

Safe 39, 91
Sampling of OnlineWomen's
   Groups, App. C 171
Self Made Man 91
Social Issues Research Center at
   Oxford 24
Society of Women Engineers 10
Starbucks 88
Stewart, Martha 27

T

"The Cellular Church" 141
"The Power of Sound" 144
thecorporation.com 46

175

The Influencers 26
The Natural Advantages of Women ii
The New Yorker Magazine 141
The New York Daily News 111
The New York Times 111
The Purpose Driven Life 43
The Washington Post 111
Thoughtful 39, 133
Time Magazine 111
Title IX 21, 22
Tomboy Tools 83
trust 1, 31, 163
Trust Barometer Report 31
Trust Point Checklists
   Community 51
   Considerate 79
   Fun 89
   Honesty 116
   Loyalty 159
   Reliable 130
   Respectful 66
   Safety 103
   Thoughtful 146
trust points 39
Tupperware 83

U

U.S. Census, gender statistics 18
U.S. Postal Service 101
Ultimate Question 34

V

VeroLabs 94
VH1 138

Vincent, Norah 91
Visionary Selling 145

W

wakati.org 145
Wal-Mart 139
Warm Kids, Inc. 142
Warren, Rick 43
What Women Really Want: How American Women are Quietly Erasing, Political, Racial, Class, and Religions Lines to Change the Way We Live Forever 61
Whirlpool Corporation 137
Whitney, Catherine 61
Why Men Don't Listen & Women Can't Read Maps 36
WomanSage ii, 8, 55
women-owned 11
women-owned business statistics 11, 20
women's business divisions at major banks 102
women's communities 41
women's culture 6
Women's Financial Network 21
Women in Cable & Telecommunications 10
Women in International Trade 10
Women in Management 10
Women Lawyers Association 10
Women Manufacturers Network 10
word-of-mouth 23, 109, 130, 159
Word-of-Mouth Glossary, App. B 169

How to Order:

Additional copies of *In Women We Trust* can be ordered online at:

www.WMEBooks.com

Or, by calling toll-free: 1-877-947-BOOK (2665)

Ask for it at your local bookstore by title, author name, or ISBN 0-9777297-2-9

For more information on quantity purchases, discounts, and special programs, please contact:

Special Book Orders
Windsor Media Enterprises, LLC
282 Ballad Avenue
Rochester, NY 14626

info@wmebooks.com

The author invites your comments. Really.

Contact her on her blog at:

www.InWomenWeTrust.com